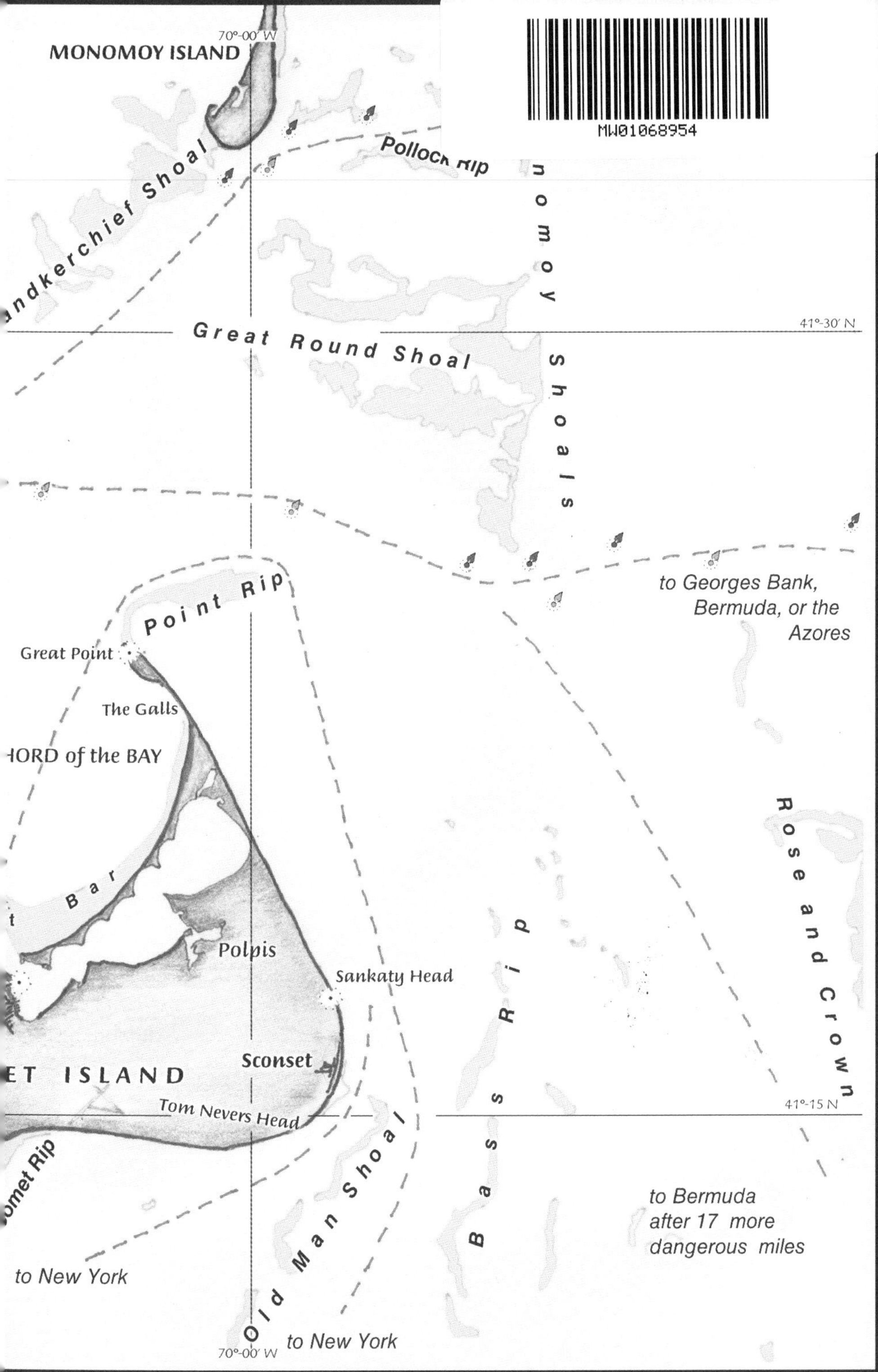

MONOMOY ISLAND

70°-00' W

ndkerchief Shoal

Polloch Rip

Great Round Shoal

n o m o y

41°-30' N

S h o a l s

Point Rip

Great Point

The Galls

HORD of the BAY

B a r

t

Polpis

Sankaty Head

ET ISLAND

Sconset

Tom Nevers Head

omet Rip

to New York

Old Man Shoal

to New York

70°-00' W

to Georges Bank,
Bermuda, or the
Azores

R o s e   a n d   C r o w n

41°-15 N

B a s s   R i p

to Bermuda
after 17 more
dangerous miles

Sailing around
NANTUCKET

✳ ✳ ✳ ✳ ✳ ✳ ✳ ✳ ✳ ✳ ✳

Sailing around
NANTUCKET

A GUIDE TO CRUISING NANTUCKET WATERS

SECOND EDITION

Alfie Sanford

TILBURY HOUSE
PUBLISHERS

Originally published by Mill Hill Press
An affiliate of the
Egan Maritime Institute
5 A Bayberry Court
Nantucket, MA 02554

www.eganmaritime.org

10   9   8   7

Copyright © 2015

Dust jacket photos by Garth Grimmer

Illustrations by Alfie Sanford

Photos on contents pages, first page, top left, photo
© Alfie Sanford; bottom right, photo © Alfie Sanford;
second page, top left, photo © Garth Grimmer, center
left, map courtesy of the Nantucket Historical
Association; center right, photo © Garth Grimmer;
bottom right, photo © Garth Grimmer.

Editor: Dick Duncan
Copyeditor: Judith Brown
Proofreader: Kate Whelan
Book design by Cecile Kaufman, X-Height Studio

ISBN: 978-0-88448-785-2

Library of Congress Control Number: 2015933167

First Tilbury House Printing 2019

Printed by Versa Press, East Peoria, IL

First Mill Hill Press printing 2015

Printed in the United States of America

Photo © Garth Grimmer

Dedicated to my father, Alfred (Teeny) Sanford,
who taught me sailing in his boat,
boatbuilding in his workshop,
and introduced me to my heroes in his library.

CONTENTS

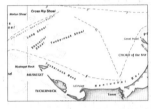
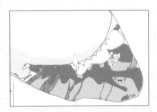

FOREWORD

Alfie sanford's *Sailing around Nantucket* is the cruising guide I wished I could have read 29 years ago when my wife Melissa and I first moved to the island. Nantucket is a beautiful place with a fascinating past, but it hides its secrets with an elaborate and sometimes intimidating care. Its harbor is one of the most beautiful in the world, but navigating a boat from the main anchorage to the harbor's eastern extreme in Wauwinet—let alone to that harbor within a harbor known as Polpis—is not easy. For the first time in the storied history of Nantucket, a mariner with an unmatched understanding of the island has produced a detailed, wonderfully written instruction manual to getting the most out of every nook and cranny—from Great Point to the east to Madaket and Tuckernuck to the west. If you live on or are visiting Nantucket and have access to a boat of any kind—whether it be a sailboat, motorboat, kayak, stand-up paddleboard, or kiteboard—this is the book for you.

I've had the pleasure of knowing Alfie Sanford for close to three decades. I've sailed with him on an Alerion—the iconic centerboard sloop based on a Nathanael Herreshoff design that Alfie has turned into a Nantucket original. The two of us have traded books about sailing and the sea and talked in detail about boat design. I crewed for Alfie during a memorable passage from Portugal to Madeira in his magnificent wooden yawl *Impala*. More recently

I've watched him create his latest floating masterpiece, the 40-foot centerboard yawl *Starry Night*. I knew that Alfie was thoughtful and wonderfully iconoclastic, combining a professorial enthusiasm for learning with the swashbuckling recklessness of a true voyager. As he freely admits, the only reason he knows the island's many shoals so intimately is that he has run aground, at one time or another, on just about every one of them. But I had no idea he was as good a writer as this book reveals him to be.

So I encourage you, one and all, to embark with Alfie on what is the voyage of a lifetime. Yes, Alfie has sailed the world's greatest oceans and visited her most exotic ports, but, as he says in the pages that follow, he has never found a place to match his homeport of Nantucket. In the tradition of Arthur Gardner's *Wrecks Around Nantucket*, Clint Andrews's *Fishing around Nantucket*, Alfie Sanford has given us yet another island classic: *Sailing around Nantucket*, a book to take with you as you guide your boat along the wave-washed shores of an island that is best appreciated by sea.

—Nathaniel Philbrick, December 2014

1

Cruising

Yawl

For it is the land that makes the yachtsman appreciate the sea...

—Carlton Mitchell, *Yachtsman's Camera*

CRUISING IS THE art of exploring the interaction of the land with the sea.

Being the record of the long game between the forces of creation and decay, the coastal edge is hugely varied. Some coasts are blessed, some are forlorn. Some edges are barren—a hard line that abruptly divides land from sea. These have but two conditions: open sea and land, separated by a surf zone. Rather than joining land and sea, they separate them.

And some edges are rich—a complex intertwining of sea with land that forms a multitude of water conditions. Between open sea and shore we find gulfs, bights, bays, islands, sounds, passages, straits, channels, coves, peninsulas, isthmuses, points, spits, lagoons, deltas, flats, creeks, and pools. These forms interest the cruiser because they join land to the sea. People have used them throughout the ages, and a rich history has developed around them.

Such are the waters of Nantucket—complex, beautiful, historical. I came to know them as a child, first wading from the beach, then sailing out upon them aboard my father's boat. A little older, I ventured forth in command of a Rainbow of my own.[1]

As a youth I felt the attraction of Nantucket's waters, but I did not understand the physical basis of my feelings. Although I sensed the fact, I did not know explicitly that shelter requires an indentation in the shoreline, and the more convoluted the concavity the better. Such a shape blocks seas and creates the possibility of a landing place. Back then, I did not see the larger picture of channels which lead from Nantucket's coves, through and around their protecting features, to landings nearby, and beyond to the open sea. But in time, I sailed farther—into the upper harbor, around to Madaket, then, out into the Sound, and, finally, through the Sound into the Atlantic to the Maritimes, to the West Indies, and to Europe.

And having returned from my voyaging I began to comprehend the significance of the land/sea interaction and the physical reasons for Nantucket's charm. I came to understand that my delight in Nantucket's waters was generated by the great variety of conditions formed by Nantucket's interaction with the sea, conditions ranging from almost landlocked, such as Polpis Harbor, to open ocean, such as off the South Shore, with a multitude of conditions in between. I came to understand that my delight also stemmed from sailing the channels that connect all these places, running from the most enclosed coves out to the open sea and accessing lands far beyond the Island. And it came from participating with sailors of the past in the ongoing story of these famous waters.

I was older when I realized that the oceans of Earth are remarkable, both because they are easy to move through and because they are interconnected. Any place at the edge of the sea—most of the world—can be reached from any other by a seaman with a boat. His only limitation is the availability of landing places. For the sailor

---

1. Rainbow is how the deservedly famous and once ubiquitous Beetle Cat is known on Nantucket.

Nantucket's wharves give access to the whole world. *Impala* sailing 3,400 miles from home at 70° north, Norway, 2004. Photo © Connor Wallace.

sails the sea to reach the land. The essence of his voyage is that it starts at a harbor where he embarks his passengers and cargo. It progresses through a channel to the open sea. It continues across the sea. It ends following another channel to a destination harbor where his passengers and cargo are discharged. The sailor can sail the sea, but at some point he must come to land, to land his passengers and cargo, restock and repair his ship. It is at a landing on the edge of the sea that each accomplished voyage begins and ends.

Blessed to learn sailing in such a fine harbor as Nantucket's, I was early unaware that the sea, so easy to move through, can be difficult to stop in. I did not know that a good harbor is a rare and fine thing that occurs only where land and sea intermingle in a particular way to satisfy several requirements.

Landing places are formed in the yin and yang interaction of land embracing sea, sea penetrating land. If the embrace is strong—deeply concave—the landing place will be protected from waves and may be suitable for a harbor. Protection from waves is the first requirement because a boat, being buoyant, moves with the surface of the sea. On a wavy surface a vessel will be in motion, not only up and down but also back and forth. She cannot be tied to a fixed structure without battering herself to pieces. So a harbor must have surrounds that stop the waves.

To be useful, a harbor must be well connected to the sea. Access to a harbor is controlled by its channel, the path of deep water around the points, shoals, and islands that separate it from the open ocean. The barriers that protect a harbor are also hazards to navigation. Landforms that can break the seas of the open ocean can also break a boat. For Nantucket, the Nantucket Bar was both protection and hazard. It protected the harbor from north winds and seas, and for 200 years it restricted entry to shoal draft vessels, a serious defect during the height of the whaling era. Only at the end of the nineteenth century did Nantucket become a deep water port, when the construction of the jetties scoured a channel through the Bar.

A harbor needs enough depth of water to float the vessels using it but not so much that they cannot anchor within it. Many a sheltered shore fails as a harbor because the bottom is too far down. This is not a problem in southern New England, but it can be in Maine and the Maritimes. Try stopping in a Norwegian fjord! Further, the bottom needs to have good holding for anchors, not too soft, not too hard. Here, Nantucket Harbor fails to some degree. The bottom in the anchorage area is soft, as a number of yachts—including the beautiful *Mistress*—found out when, in August 1953, Hurricane Carol blew them, dragging their anchors, up onto the Easton Street shore.

A good harbor lacks strong currents but has adequate flushing action to remove wastes. It will not have a great rise and fall of tide because that will complicate anchoring and make coming alongside docks difficult. It should not generate williwaws,[2] or worse, suffer seiches,[3] which will suddenly distress vessels thought to be secure.

And then there are the requirements of the land side. A harbor not only must protect from the sea but also must supply the resources of the land—provision, repair, and society.

---

2. The term *williwaw* refers to localized, sudden winds of great strength. Williwaws may be *katabatic* winds—cold air masses that "fall" down steep mountain slopes due to their weight—or they may be turbulence caused by winds around certain land forms. The winds have different names in different parts of the world, "bora" on the Adriatic, "Santa Anna" in Southern California. I use "williwaw" here generically in honor of Slocum, who memorialized the williwaws of the Magellan Straits and introduced me to the phenomenon.

3. A *seiche* is a solitary wave that will cause a sudden change in water level. Trapani and Marsala, ports at the western tip of Sicily, are famous for their seiches, which will raise the level of those harbors four to six feet in a few seconds, breaking ships free of their docks and generally creating mischief. Seiches occur in basins of particular shapes. They are caused by atmospheric conditions, and are difficult to predict.

A harbor needs to be well connected to the hinterland so that goods and travelers brought by sea can continue on their trips. Nantucket, being a small and flat island, never had a big problem with internal communications. Nonetheless, when, at the beginning of the eighteenth century, the inhabitants developed the Great Harbor, they actually moved the existing town to the new site and rebuilt it as an extension of their new wharves. The tight integration of town and harbor created a hospitable landing both for the whalers arriving from afar and for the local packets trading with the nearby mainland. Today the advantages of land/sea integration remain.

As the cruiser explores the interaction of land and sea on his particular cruising ground, his principal activity is the discovery of its harbors and passage through the channels leading into them. At the end of his day he will take delight from the protected cove into which he has found his way and in which he enjoys a night away from the tumult of the sea.

He will also enjoy a cultural aspect to his cruise. The discovered cove in which the cruiser takes his delight is, in truth, rediscovered. In his yacht, he has followed the tracks of earlier explorers' ships. His stopping place has been used, since the beginning of navigation, by other sailors. Good stopping places generate culture because a harbor begins and ends the voyages that sustain the people living there. Each voyage is an adventure; each adventure has a story. The stories join to make the people's history. Sailing around Nantucket, I gained greater understanding of its connections to the rest of the world. I began to see both its natural advantages and the difficulties people had to overcome to generate a way of life that created their commerce and culture.

Eighteenth-century Nantucket was an outcome of the age of European exploration during which sailors mastered the art of navigation to sail voyages of discovery. They explored new coasts to find convenient landings well connected to the newfound lands they sought to exploit. Subsequent adventurers developed these landings into towns and ports. Histories grew up around these places, cultures developed. Exploration was big business; fortunes were made; empires were built. In Nantucket the business was whaling. The fortunes were large.

Today empires no longer connect via the sea, but rather, through the atmosphere. The airliner has taken the place of the sailing ship, and the oceans' practical use has been downgraded to moving heavy cargoes slowly. Sail navigation for imperial exploration is gone.

But out of change and decay comes renewal. In our time, a new kind of voyage has sprung up, that of the cruising yachtsman. A cruising voyage is a new kind of voyage of exploration.

Winston Churchill said, "We shape our buildings, and afterwards our buildings shape us." He was speaking of architecture, but the same is true of landscape. We don't actually shape landscape, but we do find it, choose it, and inhabit it; then it shapes us.

The essential purpose of cruising is learning how the shape of our shore has shaped our civilization on it. A cruiser sailing around Nantucket will not find the whaling capital of the world—that is gone. He will find instead a wonderland of water, marsh, and sand that shaped the people of Nantucket into the whaling force that astonished the world. By connecting with its past, he learns the truth about its present. He learns to separate the transitory from the persistent. He learns about himself. On a small boat he learns it firsthand and in a way that is hard to forget.

The intent of this volume is to give understanding of the waters around Nantucket. I start with discussion of the natural processes that created the waterscape and its complex of patterns. I then describe the local waters by depicting the principal landing places and the channels leading to them. I indicate their cultural significance by discussing their history. Finally I discuss the boats suited to Nantucket's waters.

During a lifetime of sailing around Nantucket I have used the Island as a launch pad for many voyages to parts abroad. The voyages have been exhilarating. But, for me, the greater thrill is the return. Each return commingles in my mind with the returns of four centuries of voyaging sailors—and more, memories of my own returns as a younger man. Each trip was unique, but each had this common end. Entering Nantucket Sound is the beginning of an embrace from the Island. At first the embrace is a gentle hug by the outstretched arms of Great Point and the western islands. The embrace becomes tighter as you slide past the nautiphone at the jetty's end, first the East Jetty, then the West, protectively separating you from the sea. A mile on, Coatue brings dry land to port, and a little farther, with the Hulbert Avenue beach close on your starboard, you have come inland. Rounding the point, the embrace becomes intimate, you are out of the wilderness of the sea and home, at last, to Nantucket.

Star knot

2

To Start With

Ship

One night as he lay down to sleep, his moccasin got full of
sand. He tossed and turned and kicked, and the more he
kicked, the more sand slid into his shoes.... His feet throbbed
with pain ... with his great long legs thrashing wildly, he
hurled his moccasins in the air.

One fell into the sea not far from shore and became the Island
of Martha's Vineyard. But the other moccasin sailed high up
over the water, and sped along for miles and miles before it
finally drifted gently down upon the ocean.... The Indians
called it Nantucket, the far away island.

—Jane Tompkins, *Two Pennies Overboard*

THE CREATION OF Nantucket and its sound begins with the last
ice age. A *sound* is a partly enclosed body of water between a mainland and an off-lying island. The mainland in this case is Cape Cod
and the island is Nantucket. The backbone of Nantucket is a pile of
surface debris conveyed by the last glacier, from across continental
New England, out into the sea.

A glacier works like a conveyor belt. It carries loose material
along with it as it slowly flows downhill away from its snowfield.

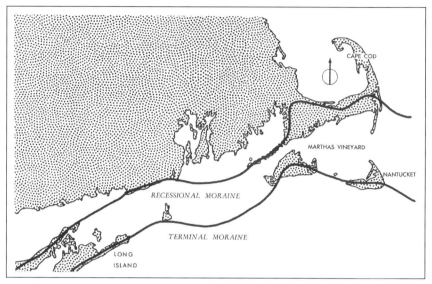

Two of the moraines left by the last glacier, forming Nantucket and its sound, speculatively 12,500 years ago.

Rather than rounding a pulley and going underground like a real conveyor belt, the glacial front gets to a point warm enough that it melts as fast as the glacier body moves it forward. The front becomes stationary. There, at its stalled edge, where the melting and forward movements are in equilibrium, all the conveyed stuff is abandoned to pile up as a moraine. The longer it stays stalled, the bigger the pile.

If the glacier speeds up or the weather gets colder, the moraine is pushed forward. If the weather warms or the glacier's movement slows, the glacier front retreats. Wherever it comes to another equilibrium, another moraine forms.

Basically, the bottom running offshore from southern New England is a sloping sand shelf. It starts about 60 feet deep along the coast and terminates about 75 to 100 miles out at the edge of the continental shelf roughly 600 feet down. It has been here a long time and was here, as the base, when the last glacier pushed its pile of detritus 30 miles beyond the continental shore and left the moraine that was to become Nantucket Island. This process is described in great and clear detail by Barbara Chamberlain in *These Fragile Outposts,* from which the chart on the preceding page is taken.[1]

Both the moraine and the bed of sand under it are malleable under the influence of wind and water. The tidal currents around the moraines are large, and their hydraulic forces are significant. The currents have sculpted this basic surface into a complex of shoals and channels. Winds and rain have shaped the land above. The result is the exquisite pattern that includes most of the possible forms of land/sea interaction—sound, bay, harbor, estuary, channel, lagoon, cove, creek, tidal pond, island, point, peninsula, bluff, dune, beach, flat.

Missing are mountains and rock. The only stones to be found in Nantucket waters are the scattered boulders dropped by the glacier and referred to as *erratics.* Well named, their positions are random, and we will find them, occasionally, as hazards to our sailing.

---

1. Chamberlain, *These Fragile Outposts,* 74.

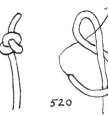

Figure eight

3

Shaping the Land and Shoals

Bark

Is there anyone who can watch without fascination the struggle for supremacy between sea and land?

The sea attacks relentlessly, marshaling the force of its powerful waves against the land's strongest points. . . .

But the land defends itself with such subtle skill that often it will gain ground in the face of the attack.

—Willard Bascom, *Waves and Beaches*

THE SANDS OF THE Sound take myriad forms, exquisite, surprising, and extremely beautiful. Being the product of natural processes, the forms are neither arbitrary nor isolated. Nor is their formation intuitive. Much is unknown about the process of their creation, and usually, in any one place, there are several basic processes occurring simultaneously that produce the complex result.

Some of the processes, however, can be considered in isolation to gain a rudimentary understanding of what is going on around Nantucket. Each particular process creates forms that are similar in structure but vary in shape and scale depending on the intensity

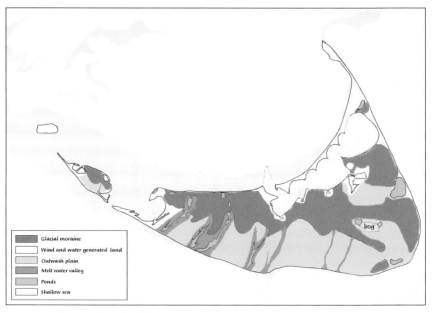

Structure of Nantucket Island

of natural forces and the boundary conditions within which they work. Most features of the waterscape about Nantucket can be understood as a combination of one or more of the four processes we will look at here.

The Crescent Beach

When an offshore wind blows into a sandy bay, the waves fan out through diffraction and spread the sand in a concentric pattern. Any small indentations tend to fill up; any protuberances are attacked and cut back. The result is a beach in a smooth crescent form. Coatue Beach is such a beach, partly formed by such action.

Barrier Bar, Barrier Beach

Barrier bars and beaches are generated by wave action perpendicular to a sandy shore. Where the shore is not subject to great rise and fall of tide, waves churn up the sand in the surf zone. The backwash current and the current induced by the incoming waves cancel each other out just beyond the surf zone, and the sand is dropped to make a bar. This bar may rise above high water to form a barrier island. From Coskata to Eel Point, Nantucket Bar is an offshore bar. Coatue is a barrier island (actually, peninsula) partly formed by such action.

Inlet Spits

Inlet spits occur where tidal flow passes between two headlands. The current running through the pass back-eddies on the downstream side of the headlands. These eddies drop suspended sand that begins spits. The spits grow out from the opposing headlands, perpendicular to the current. They narrow the opening and focus the flow into a jet, which scours a deep trough between them.

As the flow leaves the now constricted opening, the jet becomes turbulent, fans out, slows, and deposits its suspended material. Depending on the water depth and the amount of material deposited, this will form a fan of shoals in front of the opening, and tending to block it. Furthermore, there is usually wave action on the offshore side of the inlet, which also tends to push the fan back

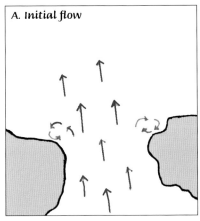
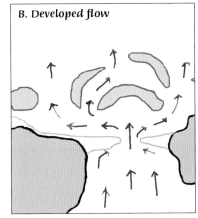

Inlet spit

into the opening. Since the water must get out, the fragments of the jet divert around the obstructions by slipping close around the ends of the spits, paralleling the shore and working their way out into the sea. Secondary jets will sometimes cut a meandering channel across the bar, but frequently these channels will die out along the way, creating dead ends and false channels.

With tidal flow, the water reverses direction and the reversed flow builds a similar structure, so the reversal reinforces and speeds up the construction of spits, often creating an obstructing fan of shoal on the inside of the opening as well. Because the water on the ocean side of the inlet is usually less obstructed and the bottom deeper, often the shoal structure on the ocean side is less developed and the shoals less shallow. At the same time, on the ocean side, the wave action is usually much stronger, so the danger greater. But each case is different, and inlets come in all different shapes and sizes. The actual configuration depends on the particulars of the headlands, water depths, and currents.

Tidal inlets and their spits are found all over Nantucket. Great Point, Coatue, Brant Point, and Smith Point are inlet spits. You can see the spits forming at the Lagoon on southeast Tuckernuck and at Eel Point. Many of the pond outlets have, or began with, this structure and have fans of shoal inside and out their entrances. The Creeks and Folgers Pond show this form, as does the cut in the East Jetty.

Longshore Transport

The movement of sand along a shore by longshore currents is known as *longshore transport.* If the currents are strong, they can move a lot of sand. They will tend to close openings and straighten shorelines. They can also create spits independent of inlets.

Along the south shore of Nantucket, the longshore currents have closed all the ponds' outlets. The ponds Miacomet, Hummock, and Long and the valley of Madequecham are the beds of old rivers, once fed by the glacier meltwaters. The ponds might have been kept open by tidal flow from inland out, as Capuam was in the early days of English settlement and as Tuckernuck's East and North Ponds are today. But longshore transport of sand along the south shore overwhelms the in-and-out cutting of the tide and quickly seals off the ponds. Occasionally storms break them open; then longshore transport quickly closes them.

Twice in recent times, storms have cut an inlet through Smith Point into Madaket Harbor. In 1961, during Hurricane Esther, Smith Point was breached to become Esthers Island with a strong current rushing through the new cut. The cut persisted for many years before longshore transport overcame its currents. The two projecting spits joined, and Smith became a point again. This cycle recurred in the 2000s. Periodically the same thing will happen at Great Point. A storm will breach the Galls and the tide will rush in and out, scouring a deep channel . . . for a while. Then the longshore transport will bring in a lot of new sand and close the beach back up.

Great Point is caused as much by longshore transport due to local tidal current anomalies as it is an inlet spit created by currents flowing in and out of Great Round Shoal Channel. Bigelows Point in Tuckernuck is due almost entirely to longshore transport.

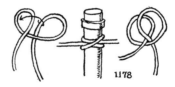

Clove hitch

4

Tides and Weather

Barkentine

Indeed, I think, that as we go on piling measurements upon measurements, and making one instrument after another more and more perfect to extend our knowledge of material things, the sea will always continue to escape us. For there is a living Spirit who rules the sea and many attendant spirits about him.

Hilaire Belloc, *The Cruise of the Nona*

THE TIDES AND THE currents they generate are the great shapers of the pile of sand we call Nantucket. They have formed many of the concavities that we use as landing places. Tide affects the depths available to our boats, and its currents affect our passage through the waters, so it is worthwhile to look at Nantucket's tides in some detail.

Fundamentally the tide is a wave generated by the gravitational pull of the sun and moon on the ocean waters. Captain Lecky explains in his famous tome:

The Tides are popularly attributed to the Moon *only*, but in point of fact they are caused by the *joint* attraction of both Sun and Moon; and it is due to this double influence, which sometimes pulls in the same and at other times in a contrary direction, that we have the ever-varying phases in the times and heights of High and Low water.

The general motion of the Tides consists in an alternate *vertical* Rise and Fall, and *horizontal* Flow and Ebb, occupying an average period of half of a lunar day, or about 12 hours 25 minutes. This vertical movement is transmitted from place to place in the seas, like an ever-recurring series of very long and swift waves.[1]

Before the specific shape of the ocean basins complicates the matter, the moon generates two bulges of water that travel around the globe under the moon during a lunar day. A lunar day is the time it takes the earth to rotate under the moon. Because the moon itself is moving in the direction of the earth's rotation (it revolves around the earth once every 28.8 days), the lunar day is about 50 minutes longer than a regular (solar) day. Since there are two bulges, the tidal cycle is about 12.4 hours long. In the deep water of the open ocean the wave is about 2 feet high and it travels about 700 knots.

But when the wave meets the land it is quite a different matter. First, in shallow water it slows down. Then it reflects off barriers and refracts around corners and diffracts through openings. In a basin of resonant proportions its height magnifies. Maybe you experienced this as a child in the bath, where, by sloshing a shallow depth of water, you could bounce a wave off the vertical face where the taps are (reflection off a barrier) and with proper timing (resonance) get it to crest over the sloping back (shallows) of the tub onto the floor—until, of course, Mother showed up.

Similar effects occur on the coast. The Irish Sea basin multiplies the oceanic tide twentyfold to a 40-foot rise and fall at Liverpool. A little farther north, the water rushes around the top of Scotland trying to fill the North Sea. There, in Pentland Firth, on a full moon night, through a channel 8 miles wide and 200 feet deep, the tidal stream reaches a velocity of 17 knots. In some places the resonance cancels out most of one of the daily tides. San Francisco Bay, like many other places, has mostly a single high and low water a day.

---

1. Lecky, "Wrinkles," in *Practical Navigation,* 182.

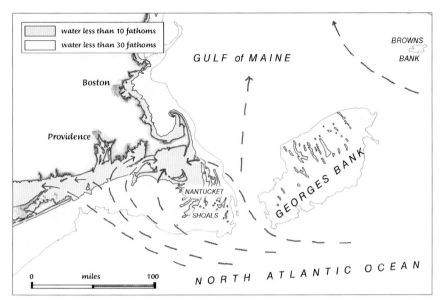

Tide coming into New England

Nantucket's waters are less extreme, but quite complicated. The tides are diurnal (two highs and lows per day), their range is from 1.5 to 5 feet, and the currents generally run about a knot, although constrictions increase them and in places they reach 4.5 knots, as in Muskeget Channel at Mutton Shoal.

To know what the tide is doing, for practical purposes it is sufficient, for the most part, to keep aboard the *Eldridge Tide and Pilot Book*, published annually since 1875. Although there are anomalies, such as those at Tuckernuck, that *Eldridge* misses, for the most part this handy volume contains the data needed to ascertain height of the water and direction of the current. Comfortable is the skipper who has his copy aboard. Incidentally, Eldridge makes a great Christmas present because you can keep giving the person who needs one a new copy each year. Really, since he needs a copy for each boat, more than one person can do this for someone with two or more boats!

To understand why the tide is doing what it is, though, we have to look a little deeper. Nantucket's tides and tidal currents are the result of three waves of tide that come together around the island. The tidal wave moves faster in deeper water. So its leading edge comes in from the open sea following the deeper channels.

The general wave moves in from the sea and divides around Nantucket Shoals. The eastern arm flows to the Gulf of Maine through Great South Channel, and some of it flows into Nantucket Sound from the east through Great Round Shoal Channel. The western arm flows into Rhode Island Sound. There it splits, one branch flowing west into Long Island Sound, the other heading back east, up Buzzards Bay, Vineyard Sound, and into Nantucket Sound from the west. A smaller portion of the western arm refracts around Nantucket Shoals and, before it gets to Rhode Island, flows into the Sound through the openings at Tuckernuck and Muskeget. This results in three wave systems interfering with each other around Nantucket.

The two major wave systems, the Martha's Vineyard and Great Round Shoal waves, meet each other head on and create a pattern of nodes and crests. The wave coming in around Tuckernuck hits the other two as a cross wave and creates peculiar tidal anomalies at the west end of Nantucket. In all, the tide creates an extremely complex pattern of high and low water and associated currents around the Island.

Two charts created by Alfred Redfield illustrate the tide and its flow around Nantucket.[2] The first shows "co-range lines." Co-range lines connect points with the *same height* of tide; the numbers represent, in feet, the difference in the heights of high and low water.

The second chart shows "co-tidal lines." Co-tidal lines connect those points where the tide is high at the *same time*. The numbers indicate occurrence of high water in hours after meridian passage of the moon. "Meridian passage," as used by Redfield, is the time of

2. Redfield, *Journal of Marine Research*, 1953. These charts and an explanation of them along with original work were given to me by Richard Limeburner of Woods Hole Oceanographic Institute, January 2014.

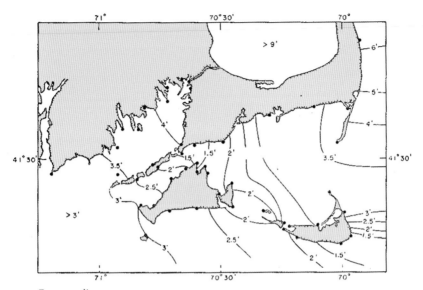

Co-range lines

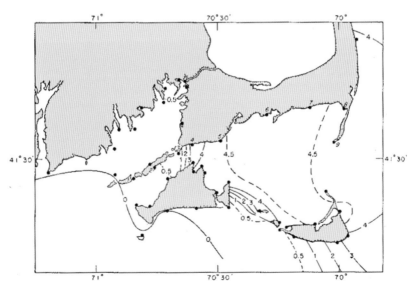

Co-tidal lines

the passing of the moon across the Greenwich meridian, or zero degrees longitude. To correct the chart to local meridian passage (70 degrees west), to when the moon is due south of us, just subtract 4.8 hours from Redfield's numbers.

The co-range chart shows that the tidal wave, as it moves past Cape Cod into the Gulf of Maine, increases rapidly in height, resulting in 9-foot tides north of the Cape (and 40-foot tides in the Bay of Fundy) compared with only 3.5-foot tides south of the Cape. In fact, the wave moves into Nantucket Sound 3.5 feet high in the east and dwindles to only 1.5 feet at Woods Hole before increasing again as it moves down Vineyard Sound. What is happening is that the flood coming in past Monomoy Island meets the ebb of the wave coming up from Newport through Vineyard Sound, and they partly cancel each other out. The chart clearly shows the node (low point) between Woods Hole and Falmouth. The same sort of interference is happening at Tuckernuck in a more complicated way.

The timing of high tide is also affected by the interaction of the different tidal waves. This is shown by the co-tidal chart. The bulk of Nantucket Sound has high tide at the same time, basically when the moon is due south. But this changes rapidly near Woods Hole and Tuckernuck, where the time of high tide shifts as much as four hours.

Richard Limeburner, of the Woods Hole Oceanographic Institute, to whom I am indebted for much of the information in this chapter, has done some original and revealing private survey work around Tuckernuck. He has found tidal differences between the north and south shores of Tuckernuck of 4.5 hours and 1.7 feet. At the west end of Bigelows Point, he found the tide quite indeterminate, with times of high tide as much as 3 hours off the lunar cycle. Its irregular rise and fall is as much as 3 feet less than it is 2 miles down the beach. As you can imagine, these variations of height and time of high tide cause strong and irregular currents around Tuckernuck.

Redfield's chart does not show co-tidal lines within Nantucket Harbor, but if it did, it might show the tide wave progressing from the mouth of the jetties up the harbor toward Wauwinet. I am unaware of any authority publishing figures for this wave, but the accepted lore has it that high tide at Wauwinet is about an hour after Brant Point, or two hours after Boston.

Redfield's charts do show the rapid change in co-range on the outside of Nantucket from Sconset to Squam. High tide is about the same time all along this stretch of beach—at meridian passage. But the rise is 1.5 feet at Sconset and 3.0 feet two miles up the beach at Squam. This generates a longshore current that is, oddly, both perpendicular to the incoming wave and strongest at times of high and low tide, normally time of slack water. Slack water here comes at mid-tide when the water levels at Squam and Sconset are equal.

The same thing occurs through Woods Hole, and for the same reason. Vineyard Sound and Buzzards Bay have the same time of high water, but due to Buzzards Bay's greater range of tide, at both high and low water, the water levels of bay and sound differ by 15 inches. A lot of water surges through the holes as it seeks its own level. The maximum current is again at times of high and low water, normally slack water.

A sailor wants to know what the actual currents are doing. At any one place and time, what are their direction and strength? Nantucket Sound in the nineteenth and early twentieth centuries was a busy and important thoroughfare. During that time extensive measurements were taken from the many lightships in the area. In 1938 the U.S. government published an atlas of tidal currents for the waters from Newport to Pollock Rip Channel. The lightship records must have been augmented by more local data because the charts are both detailed and accurate and cover a lot more ground than just the localities of the 10 lightships in the area. Although the government atlas is out of print, the charts are published in smaller format each year in *Eldridge,* which is worth its cost just for these charts.

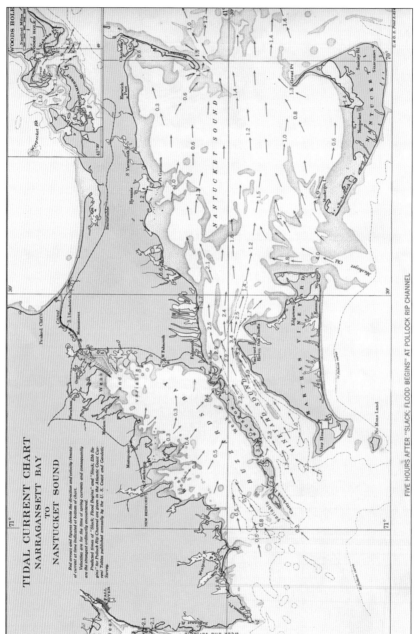

Nantucket Sound at flood tide

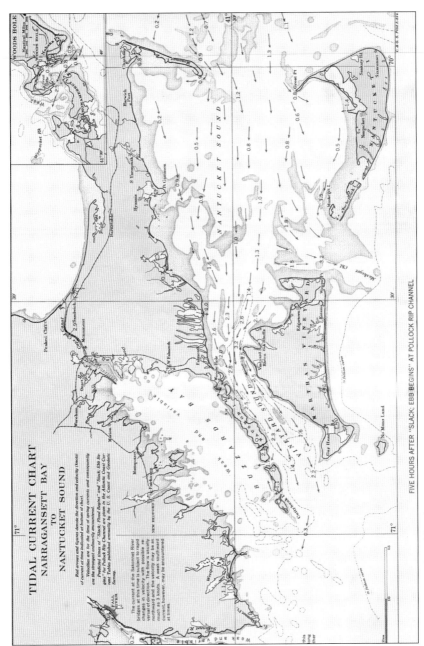

Nantucket Sound at ebb tide

To my knowledge, no formal study has been done of currents within Nantucket Harbor or around the western islands. This volume includes an informal chart of the harbor with my best guess of the currents for flood and ebb, but they should not be taken as gospel truth.

A sailor wants to know the actual depth of the water. In the shoal waters of Nantucket, three feet of tidal rise and fall can make a big difference. Only a kayak will enter Coskata Pond or the Creeks at low water, whereas a good size boat can do so at high water. The state of the tide may be important for your reputation if you become stranded aground. On a rising tide you will be off quickly and home for dinner. On a falling tide you, or at least your boat, will be indisposed for a while. Rescue may be required; explanations will be in order.

The state of tide determines the direction and strength of the currents, which run hard enough to matter to the small boats in which you will want to cruise Nantucket. With exceptions like the ones discussed above, high and low water are generally times of slack current. At other times the current may speed you on your way or hold you up. In a sailing boat, in light air, the prudent mariner will begin his trip out sailing up current so that, if becalmed, he can drift home with the tide.

Finally, the state of the tide radically changes the appearance of the waterscape. The cleanness of the full tide marsh contrasts with the muddy liveliness of low-water flats.

All of this requires knowing when high tide actually is. Good tide tables are available for Nantucket, in *Eldridge,* on calendars, and, of course, on the Internet.[3] But the more independent of mind can predict the time of high water by watching the moon.

---

3. One of the NOAA master stations for New England is established on Nantucket's Steamboat Dock. The readings from this station are combined with a tidal prediction and the results posted graphically and numerically on http://tidesandcurrents.noaa.gov/waterlevels.html?id=8449130.

Remember, it is the moon that pulls the water to make the tide and, generally, high is when the moon passes by due south of you. When the moon is in the east or west, when it is rising or setting, it will usually be close to low tide. When the moon is high overhead, it will be high tide.

The co-tidal charts give the time that is added to time of lunar passage to get time of high tide, wherever you might be. The state of the tide is not exactly in phase with the moon because the sun affects it also. But the chart will give you a time accurate to about plus or minus a half hour. This is close enough.

It is worth noting here that most of the change in tide level—71 percent—occurs during the mid three hours of the cycle. This means that at Nantucket, with its three-foot tide range, the water level will be within five inches of its high point for three hours across the high tide. Likewise, it will be within five inches of its low point for three hours across low tide. Most of the time it is either high water or low water.

Weather

Let's heed Melville's imperative and look at where Nantucket is on the map. There Nantucket is, as he says, occupying a "real corner on the world,"[4] and you can see how close it is to that "river in the ocean"[5]—the Gulf Stream—much closer than the New England and mid-Atlantic mainland. Nantucket's atmosphere is turbulent; its weather is difficult to predict. Proximity to the Gulf Stream is the reason.

Nantucket lies in the westerlies. Its prevailing winds are southwest in summer, northwest in winter. Essentially Nantucket's weather is caused by cold air from Canada flowing south-eastward to meet warm air heated by the hot waters of the Gulf Stream. The

---

4. Melville, *Moby Dick*, beginning of chapter 14.
5. Maury, *The Physical Geography of the Sea*, 1.

Ben Franklin's Gulf Stream. Courtesy of the Nantucket Historical Association.

meeting of hot and cold spawns all sorts of disturbances which start at Hatteras and move up the hot/cold interface to Nantucket.

Lt. M. F. Maury, in his magnificent *Physical Geography of the Sea,* explained the situation in 1883:

> Several years ago, the British Admiralty set on foot inquiries as to the cause of the storms in certain parts of the Atlantic, which so often rage with diasterus [sic] effects to navigation. The results may be summed up in the conclusion to which the investigation led: that they are occasioned by the irregularity between the temperature of the Gulf Stream and of the neighboring regions, both in the air and in the water. . . .
>
> . . . One of the poles of maximum cold is, according to this theory, situated in latitude 80° north, longitude 100° west. It is distant but

little more than two thousand miles, in a northwesterly direction, from the summer heated waters of this stream. This proximity of extremes of the greatest cold and summer heat will, as observations are multiplied and discussed, be probably found to have much to do with the storms that rage with such fury on the left side of the Gulf Stream.[6]

In winter, polar outbreaks send strong bitter winds down from the northwest. They meet the warm sea at Hatteras and form a front with cyclonic winds swirling around tight lows that move up the edge of the stream.

The common track takes them over Georges Bank just 120 miles east of Nantucket before they move east to the Grand Banks and on to Ireland. Sometimes they wobble west of course and run right over the Island, or occasionally go inland.

The usual track is to the east of Nantucket, causing the classic "nor'easter." This wind starts with a light easterly that shifts northeast and intensifies to gale or storm force with rain or snow. It will blow for a day or two, then move on, clearing and cooling with a northwest wind that is frequently stronger than the gale that preceded it. There may be several lows generated by a single interaction of Canadian and Gulf Stream air. They head up the western edge of the Stream towards Nantucket like a series of bullets fired from a gun. Any single low will pass by in a day, but a series can keep the nor'easter going for several days.

For summer nor'easters, the same pattern holds, but the temperature differences are not so extreme, causing the disturbances to be weaker. Summer nor'easters are generally force 6 or 7 with a short spell of northwest force 6 on the clearing side. Often they will be shorter and weaker, sometimes even without rain.

The other common condition that frequents Nantucket's waters is more general to the New England coast. A cold front moving

6. Ibid., 48.

in from Canada will cross the Island on its way out to sea. Before the cold front the wind will be warm, southerly, and moist—often foggy. After frontal passage, the wind shifts to a cool, dry northwesterly. In winter the systems are robust and often have gales on both sides of the front. In summer things are gentler. Before the front the southerly might blow as much as force 6 for a day or even two; after it the northwesterly dies to force 4 after a few hours. If the system is weak, as is likely in summer, the cold air may warm up over the Stream and return as a warm front with new southerlies and rain. Often the wind is light but rarely is it calm in Nantucket.

The prudent mariner will watch the weather forecast and not pay too much attention to it more than 48 hours out. The weatherman is often, if not usually, wrong, not because he is stupid, but because the weather in Nantucket is hard to predict. Weather is unstable in Nantucket. We are in the turbulent zone where small forces effect large changes. The particular interchange of hot and cold changes the severity of the systems. The particular track of a low center radically changes the wind direction, wind strength, cloud cover, humidity, and precipitation. Pity the weatherman.

All this said, Nantucket is blessed with good sailing weather from June till October. The typical breeze is west, starting at force 3 in the morning, shifting southwest and building with the sea breeze to force 5 in the afternoon. By evening its force falls to zero to 2. At midnight it will come up as a force 4 northerly that moderates and backs as the sun comes up. Ahh, summer . . .

Summer thunderstorms are frequently forecast for the waters, but they are actually quite rare. They try to work their way out from the overheated mainland, but the Sound waters temper them and they generally dissipate before reaching Nantucket.

Fog is frequent. The water to the east, fed by the Labrador Current, is much colder than the Sound waters and the waters southwest of the Island. When the warm moist southwesterly hits this colder water, it becomes fog. On a clear day in Nantucket, you can often see a purple bank of fog just beyond Great Point or Siascon-set. Frequently the heat of the land will lose out and fog will fill the Sound, cover the airport, and envelop the harbor with its thick wrap that makes the world quiet, and so much bigger.

Rolling hitch

5

Nantucket Sound

Brig

> There are many and dangerous shoals surrounding the
> Island and constituting a very serious menace to an unskilled
> navigator, and many a mariner has been entangled in their
> intricacies and lost his vessel on the shores of Nantucket.
>
> —Alexander Starbuck, *The History of Nantucket*

Nantucket sound has a sandy base about 60 feet deep. On top of this base, shoals have been overlaid by glacial deposits and tidal deposits bringing the bottom, in places, to within a foot of the surface. These shoals regulate the Sound's traffic.

Through the eighteenth, nineteenth, and early twentieth centuries the Sound was an important commercial waterway. As an indication of the traffic, in the early 1840s, records show about 12,000 ships, brigs, schooners, and sloops passed by Cross Rip lightship in the course of a year.[1] This is an average of a vessel every 45 minutes, 365 days a year, 24 hours a day. Lightships were stationed in as many as six different locations in the Sound, marking key bounds to the channels. Knowledge of the location, shape, and depth of the shoals was, and still is, necessary for successful navigation in the

---

1. Stackpole, *Lifesaving—Nantucket,* 93.

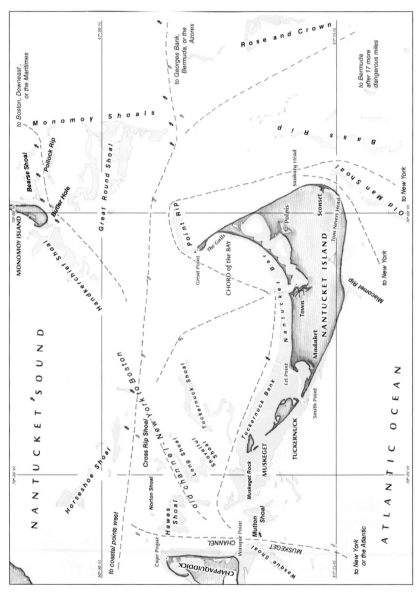

The Sound and its shoals

Sound. Interestingly, for the most part, the shoals, though made of shifting sand, persist in depth, shape, and location.

I first learned the shoals sailing Yankee One Designs across the Sound. As teenagers we day-raced these 30-foot keel boats out of the harbor in the near environs of Nantucket. Once a summer, we sailed them across the Sound to Martha's Vineyard for Edgartown's annual regatta. Yankees draw 4.5 feet and do not have engines. Running aground out of sight of land on the shoals beyond Tuckernuck could be serious. My skipper was cautious; we stuck to the buoyed channel. On later crossings, we explored the edge of the shoals, cutting some of the corners. Then, with the fearlessness of youth, we sailed a straight line across the shoals and found they were mostly deep water. Only later did I study the Sound's shoal waters and learn their patterns, which told me where the shallow (and dangerous) spots actually are.

To a great extent the shoals can be understood as the construct of tidal current processes working around the remains of the glacial moraine. They are more persistent than you would think because the tidal currents follow flow patterns dictated by the position and shapes of the moraines. Since the glacial moraines change slowly, the shoals change slowly.

In Nantucket Sound there are three systems involved, with the water flowing in and out from three major openings: in the east between Monomoy Island and Great Point, in the west between West Chop and Woods Hole, and in the south through Muskeget Channel. Water flows through the opening to the west as in a river—it passes through the Sound constrained and continues its narrow flow till it enters the sea through the eastern opening. Water flows through the openings to the east and south as tidal inlets, slowing and fanning out to create the usual pattern of shoals and channels.

The three systems set up their own patterns, but they also complicate things by interfering with each other. Still, using the general models, we can make some sense of the shoals in Nantucket Sound.

To the east the currents have created the typical inlet spits of Great Point and Monomoy Island. The opening is wide, so its obstructing fan, the Monomoy Shoals, is not very shallow but does plug up the middle of the opening. The sea pushes the shoals back, forming a distinct bar at their eastern, ocean, edge. As expected, the deepest channels are close to the ends of the spits. Pollock Rip Channel reaches an extreme depth of 114 feet in Butler Hole at the tip of Monomoy and then shoals rapidly east of Monomoy. There is a 15-foot channel leading north right along the Monomoy shore out to deep water. The bigger, marked channel carries about 25 feet but skirts shoals for 5 miles before reaching deep water to the east.

On the southern side of the opening, Great Round Shoal Channel is a continuation of the riverine channel that started in Vineyard Sound. It ends in the sea east of Nantucket. It leaves Nantucket Sound close by Point Rip and meanders through the blocking Monomoy Shoals for 12 miles before entering the deep water to the east.

Muskeget Channel, to the south, is also a tidal inlet. Its spits, Wasque Shoals on the west and Mutton Shoal/Muskeget Banks on the east, are underdeveloped and mostly underwater, perhaps because of the shape of the moraine and the interference of the water flowing in and out from the west at Cape Pogue. Similar to Butler Hole there is a deep hole, 163 feet deep, just west of Mutton Shoal. Muskeget Channel's obstructing fan, the Hawes/Tuckernuck Shoal complex, plugs the middle of the opening. As one would expect, the channels run along either side, north-south up the Chappaquiddick shore and east-west along the north edge of Tuckernuck Bank. The large riverine flow of water coming in from the west north of Cape Pogue, forming the main channel, terminates the fan shoals—Hawes, Norton, Cross Rip, and Tuckernuck— along its southern edge.

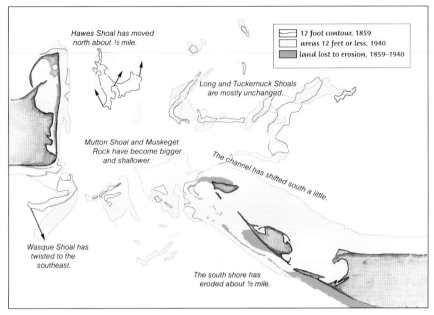

Hawes Shoal has moved
north about ½ mile.

	12 foot contour, 1859
	areas 12 feet or less, 1940
	land lost to erosion, 1859–1940

Long and Tuckernuck Shoals
are mostly unchanged.

Mutton Shoal and Muskeget
Rock have become bigger
and shallower.

The channel has shifted south a little.

Wasque Shoal has
twisted to the
southeast.

The south shore has
eroded about ½ mile.

Persistence of shoals

The pattern of the shoals is complex, but it is persistent. Navigators of the nineteenth century knew their names and would find them much the same today. Although the sands are volatile, easily moved by storms and surges, the pattern of the shoals remains year after year essentially unchanged. If disturbed, after a short time, the pattern reforms. The Hawes/Tuckernuck Shoal complex shows on the chart of 1859 with essentially the same shape and depth as today. It has moved north about half a mile, consistent with the northerly retreat of the south shores of Nantucket and Tuckernuck. Likewise, Great Point has been cut off at the Galls to form an island several times over the past four centuries. Each time it quickly reforms. The details of the inlet shoals and channel will change with each storm. But these structures are built by the currents. As long as the water continues to flow and the headlands remain, they will persist in general shape, position, and depth.

The illustration shows the surveys from 1859 and 1940 overlaid. The Hawes/Tuckernuck Shoal complex is nearly identical except that it has moved about a half mile to the northeast. Katama, Tuckernuck, and Smith Point, the bases around which the currents flow, have eroded about the same amount. As the headlands change, the shoals change with them. But the pattern persists.

It is worth taking a minute to discuss the principal channels through and into the Sound, because the channels organize the navigation. There are four routes from afar to Nantucket, all across Nantucket Sound: west through Vineyard Sound, south through Muskeget Channel, east through Great Round Shoal Channel, and north or east through Pollock Rip Channel.

My older readers will remember the western channel from riding the steamers from Woods Hole and New Bedford to Nantucket. When I was young my family traveled to Nantucket from Tennessee each June. We traveled by air. On one trip we started in bright sunshine in Knoxville at 8:00 a.m., and about 5:00 p.m. we landed in heavy fog in New Bedford, 950 miles from home and 50 miles short of Nantucket. We stayed at the Sanford Hotel, and I remember being unconvinced, at age seven, that the name was coincidental. The ice cream cones cost 15 cents, which my elders thought exorbitant but figured it was part of the cost of a summer in New England.

It was just as foggy the next morning, so we abandoned the air and embarked on the steamship *Nobska* for the five-hour voyage to Nantucket with a stop in Woods Hole. Halfway from Woods Hole to Nantucket, we came to the *Cross Rip* light vessel, gave it a toot, and changed course for Nantucket. A light vessel no longer marks the northern edge of Tuckernuck Shoal, but the shoal remains as the principal obstruction around which the route to and from the westward bends.

Although I never again sailed from New Bedford, I made the trip many times in fair weather and foul from Woods Hole until the route was abandoned commercially in the 1970s. The important waypoint was Cross Rip Shoal. When I was young it had a lightship, later just a red and a black (now green) bell that the steamer passed between and turned southeast for the last leg into Nantucket. My father had a framed picture of Cross Rip hanging in his library in Tennessee. It meant little to my friends, but to me, it meant coming to Nantucket.

The channel from the west is the coastwise route. Nantucket Sound is the northeastern end of an intra-coastal waterway system of semi-protected water that runs all the way from Texas. It starts in Brownsville and runs behind Padre Island to Corpus Christi, behind Matagorda Island to Galveston, across the Sabine River to Morgan City, and up to New Orleans. From there it crosses Lake Pontchartrain to Biloxi, Mobile, Pensacola, turning southeast to Panama City and Tampa, Florida. It traverses the Florida peninsula via canal and Lake Okeechobee and progresses up the East Coast behind a string of barrier islands past Jacksonville, Savannah, and Charleston, inside the fearsome Carolina Capes to the Chesapeake Bay at Norfolk. The route passes Baltimore, crosses to Delaware Bay at Wilmington, and turns south to Cape May before continuing north up the Jersey Shore. The route loses protection of the barrier islands at Manasquan Inlet. From Manasquan it runs a very exposed 25 miles before entering New York Harbor. Protected once more, the channel continues up the East River, past Manhattan, out through Hell Gate into Long Island Sound. It leaves the sound through The Race and has another 30-mile exposed stretch until it enters Buzzards Bay. From Buzzards Bay it passes through Woods Hole, across Vineyard Sound, past West Chop, East Chop, and Cape Pogue. Then after Cross Rip it turns southeast around Tuckernuck Shoal and into Nantucket Harbor. This 3,000-mile channel links all the great ports of Atlantic America and ends in Nantucket. To go farther, one braves the Atlantic.

To go Down East from Nantucket—which from Nantucket is actually up north—one uses Pollock Rip Channel. It is well marked with a line of red nuns and bells on the Handkerchief Shoal side and cans marking Stone Horse Shoal on the east. The issue in the summer is usually fog. The water just outside the Cape is cold, and many times I have sailed through Butler Hole in bright sunshine, clearly seeing the tip of Monomoy Island, and sailed into a wall of fog a quarter-mile off the beach. Bearse Shoal is a hazard, often marked by breakers, and you are not out to sea till you're five miles on past red gong "4," from whence you are clear to sail to Boston, Portland, or Halifax, the three Atlantic ports beyond the intra-coastal waterway.

The main channel east to Georges Bank continues straight past Cross Rip and by Great Point through the Great Round Shoal Channel. Great Round, again, is well marked, and in the past it needed no light vessels. It bends north a little to miss Point Rip and then south to clear the south end of Great Round Shoal almost seven miles out from Great Point. The channel is wide and easier than Pollock Rip to its north. Fog clings here as well but is not as sudden as with Pollock Rip.

Past Great Round Shoal, if you continue east and follow the buoyed channel for another 10 miles, you come to the open water of the Great South Channel, which you really should do if you are headed to Bermuda. Even then you do not really clear Nantucket Shoals till you have passed Asia Rip another 45 miles on. These are the famous Nantucket Shoals, which have wrecked so many ships. They are the first obstruction forming the channel leading to the Port of New York from northern Europe.

When we were young and a little foolish we would sail our cruising boats south to the West Indies for the winter. The procedure was to wait till the hurricanes died down and leave Nantucket in November. November in New England is winter time; the weather is strong and the water cold. One would wait till a cold front had passed through and then set out on its back side. November 1975 was no exception. We got the sloop, *Piera,* under way about 2:00 p.m. The sun had set as we passed Great Point. It was getting dark.

The wind was a brisk force 6 northwester. We cleared green bell "7" just beyond Point Rip and bore away to the southeast figuring to sail down the narrow channel between Bass Rip and Rose and Crown Shoal. This was long before GPS, but the visibility was good and Sankaty was blinking away every 7.5 seconds. Great Point light was visible astern. I had the deck, and the rest of the crew were down below preparing dinner. I had my hands full steering, and it was too cold to fool with taking a lot of cross bearings, so I sailed my compass course, enjoying the waves rushing up astern and passing by us with their swoosh and foam. Until they were not coming up from astern. I was sitting there at the helm steering when a series of breaking waves swept the boat from over the bow, directly against the wind. They filled the cockpit and my boots with clean cold Labrador Current seawater.

It did not last long, four waves I think, but it did inspire me to take bearings on Great Point and Sankaty to find out, fast, just exactly where we were. We were about 100 yards on the far side of Rose and Crown Shoal, whose granite, in places, comes to within 4 feet of the surface.

It turned out we had drifted off course to the east and right across the shoal. What happened? Well, in the rush to get to sea, the skipper had stowed the outboard motor in the cockpit locker about three feet from the compass, and our deviation at the moment was 15 degrees.

The sailing moral is, mind your compass, but the issue for this book is that the Nantucket Shoals are dangerous and extensive. They are not that easy to sail through even in a shoal draft yacht. I learned this again in 1990 aboard *Impala*. I left again in the fall, this time October, bound for Cape May, New Jersey. There were just two of us aboard, and the wind was northwest again, not so strong. I wanted to get to sea quickly because we were shorthanded. *Impala* had no autopilot, and I did not want to spend a lot of time navigating in close waters. So, eschewing the western route through

Vineyard Sound, we ran to Great Point, turned south right after the rip, and headed for Tom Nevers Head. The actual situation looks different in what my children called "real life" than it does on the chart. I learned the hard way how much shoal water there is to avoid to get by Tom Nevers Head. Coming from the north, there is a narrow channel that can take you inside Old Man Shoal just west of Sconset. But it is not all that easy to find the entrance. I played it safe and chose, when I got there, to go outside Old Man. The problem then was to know when you are clear of Old Man at its southwest end. There is no mark to tell you when you are through, and it is a good 5 miles to open water. Safely beyond Old Man we had sailed 17 miles from Point Rip to the open ocean, always within a mile or so of shallow water. We were glad to have finally cleared it to settle down to an open passage to New Jersey. Today with GPS it would be much easier.

I did not know it then, but a better way for us to have gone would have been through Muskeget Channel. Muskeget Channel remains today the least known and least used route in and out of Nantucket Sound. It is direct, short, and, in the right conditions, the easiest way to points south of the Island. The main channel goes by Cross Rip on the way to the westward, then turns south at green bell "21A" off Cape Pogue and runs down the Chappaquiddick shore straight to sea past Mutton Shoal. It is well marked and the current runs with the direction of the channel, so it is easy to remain in the channel, even in fog.

I took this route when *Impala* was leaving Nantucket in May 2011 bound for Gibraltar. We had waited out most of a six-day nor'easter. But it was still blowing hard, force 7. It was cold. Although we were headed east in general, I looked forward to reaching the warmer water of a Gulf Stream meander just 75 miles south of Nantucket. The prospect of beating out 30 miles of Great Round Shoal Channel was unattractive, and I was aware of the difficulty of getting south directly from Great Point. So we left Nantucket at

11:00 a.m. with double-reefed main and staysail and beat to Tuckernuck bell. There we eased off a little, passed Cross Rip, and at Cape Pogue turned to run down the Chappaquiddick shore. We passed Mutton Shoal and Wasque Island, our last sight of land for 17 days. We reached the outer bell "MC" and deep water at 2:00 p.m. At 2:00 a.m. the next morning the wind had eased and the water temperature had risen 25 degrees since midnight to 70 degrees.

It is a good way out and, if you go the long way around Tuckernuck Shoals, easy enough even for gale conditions, as we had, or in poor visibility. In easier conditions there are two alternative channels. The most direct leads from the Nantucket Bar bell west to the Eel Point bell, continuing on past the northwest corner of Muskeget to a point near the Muskeget Channel nun "4." From there you turn south to go past Mutton Shoal and out to sea. This way is about 22 miles from Nantucket Harbor to deep water, much the most direct way south and west.

As the channel passes the northwest corner of Muskeget there is a narrow spot between Tuckernuck Bank and the bottom end of Tuckernuck Shoal. The edge of the bank is usually easily seen, but the shoal to the north is not. I have sailed through here maybe ten times and have seen no sign of the four-foot depth marked on the chart. I wonder if it actually exists. Also, the turning point where you make your turn to Mutton Shoal is unmarked. With GPS it is easy enough to set up a waypoint here, and you do not have to be too accurate because there is a good bit of room. You must be careful to miss the shoal northwest of Bass Ledge. Usually it breaks and is visible.

There is another route through Tuckernuck Shoals that intrigues me, but I have never used it, nor know anyone who has. If you plot a line from Cross Rip Shoal nun "4" to Muskeget Channel nun "4" off the Chappaquiddick shore, you will see a deep channel with Norton and Hawes Shoals to the west and Long Shoal to the east. Coming in through Pollock Rip Channel and going out this way would be a direct route for a vessel wanting to use Nantucket Sound to bypass Nantucket Shoals on the way from Down East to New York. I wonder if the position of these two buoys is coincidental or if it is a vestigial remain from nineteenth-century buoyage of this channel. The chart of 1858 shows a buoy at the northeastern extremity of Long Shoal. If that buoy were still there it would make the channel easy to follow. The same chart shows buoys marking the northern corners of Hawes Shoal and the west side of Bass Ledge, which indicates to me that this way to Muskeget Channel was well known and well used back then.

Anchor hitch

6

Nantucket Island

Schooner

Would you believe that a sandy spot, of about twenty-three
thousand acres, affording neither stones nor timber,
meadows nor arable, yet can boast of an handsome town
consisting of more than 500 houses, should possess above
200 sail of vessels, constantly employ upwards of 2000 seamen,
feed more than 15,000 sheep, 500 cows, 200 horses; and has
several citizens worth more than £20,000 sterling!

—J. Hector St. John de Crèvecoeur,
commenting on Nantucket Island sometime
before 1783, *Letters from an American Farmer*

THE CHANNELS OF Nantucket Sound lead to Nantucket Island.
This lump of glacial debris, 30 miles from the mainland and the
closest point on the American shore to the Gulf Stream and the
shipping lanes to Europe, has a lot of history packed into its 50
square miles.

The Island has two distinct sides. The north side, facing and
enclosing the Sound, is strongly concave. The south and east sides
of the Island are strongly convex. The Island projects its back into
the hard North Atlantic while opening its arms to embrace the

softer waters of Nantucket Sound. At age eight my little sister pro-
nounced Nantucket shaped like a lamb chop. There is truth to what
she said.

Concavity makes for landing places, and when the Europeans
came to Nantucket, in the mid-seventeenth century, they came
ashore at Warren's Landing, a protected spot in Madaket Harbor.
They then moved east from Warren's Landing to the completely
sheltered and tiny Capuam Pond. At that time Capuam Pond was
open to the sea, perhaps as East Pond of Tuckernuck is today. Their
boats were small and the convenience of the location great. But
Capuam Pond could harbor little more than beach boats.

About 1700, after 50 years of indifferent agriculture, the people
of Nantucket took the art of beach whaling to sea. By 1720 they
had perfected offshore whaling. To accommodate their expand-
ing ambitions, Nantucketers developed the Great Harbor with a
complex of wharves suitable for the radical new technology of offshore whaling and the international commerce that went with it.
For the next 120 years Nantucket, a town of 5,000, dominated the
worldwide whaling industry, established colony ports in four for-
eign countries, became the major player in the Western discovery
of the Pacific, and was one of the richest societies on earth. It came
to an end suddenly in the 1840s with the advent of the railroad,
discovery of oil, and competition from New Bedford, a Nantucket
whaling colony established by William Rotch in 1765.

Finally, the great fire of 1846, which destroyed the downtown area,
brought the whaling era to an end. Although the downtown was
partially rebuilt and several new mansions constructed on upper
Main Street after the fire, the industry never recovered. Nantucket
whaling was over. The entrepreneurs dispersed. Many joined the
China trade; others went to San Francisco and were involved with
the gold rush. Macy's left Main Street and went to New York City.
A generation later, Nantucket was a sleepy "fish" town. Its reduced

population was predominantly Azoreans and Cape Verdeans, who came ashore from the Grand Banks cod fish grounds.

Inevitably the industrial gentry of twentieth-century America discovered Nantucket. Slowly, at first, Nantucket developed as a summer resort. The growth accelerated in the 1980s and 1990s, so today Nantucket for the second time is a wealthy place with an eclectic mix of the world's peoples walking its streets.

I think the waters attracted them here. Here perched on the northwest edge of the fearsome and majestic Atlantic Ocean is a most exquisite intertwine of land and sea, whether presented in bright sparkling sunlight or in a vapor of fog. The water is warm, the beaches are ubiquitous. Neither the island nor beaches remain empty, however. Nantucket's empty spaces have filled in during the past 30 years, so it is more like Bermuda than the quiet place it was for 100 years after the collapse of the whaling industry. Nonetheless, its eighteenth-century town, built by the whalers, is still the best small urbanization in the United States, and the island offers the best sailing in the world.

Four regions make up the sailing grounds of Nantucket Island: Chord of the Bay, Nantucket Harbor, Up Harbor, and the West End. Each will be discussed in detail in one of the next four chapters. I'll describe their various landing spots and the channels leading to them.

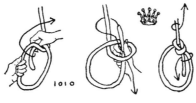

Bow line

7

Chord of the Bay

Sloop

> Though we still have some fishing boats and fisheries, most
> fishing today is done mechanically and does not make for
> interesting scenes.
>
> —J. Clinton Andrews, *Fishing Around Nantucket*

CHORD OF THE Bay is the great arc of water embraced by Great
Point and Coatue. The name does not show up on the charts, but
as Stackpole says, the name has been used for centuries.[1] Chord of
the Bay was, and is, a general anchorage area, and for a vessel large
enough to deal with the chop on the Sound it is a good one, protection from the east being available by the lee of Great Point and from
the south and west from Coatue and the East Jetty. Only from the
northwest is it open; even large vessels would not want to anchor
here in a northwest gale. The eastern portion of Chord of the Bay is
deep; 50 feet of water comes in close to the beach. The southwest-
ern corner contains the eastern bit of Nantucket Bar and is shallow
in close. In a summer southwesterly, small craft can take shelter in

---

1. Stackpole, *Lifesaving—Nantucket, 43*.

the lee of the East Jetty if awaiting a better time to enter Nantucket Harbor. Chord of the Bay has three special stopping places, and I discuss them as follows.

Great Point and the Galls

APPROACH: One generally approaches Great Point from the southwest through deep water (some of the deepest in the Sound, 50-plus feet) right up to the beach. There are no offshore hazards, and it will be too deep to anchor until you are close into shore.

BOTTOM: The bottom is sandy. Good holding.

CURRENTS: There is some current here, northwesterly with the flood, southeasterly with the ebb.

PROTECTION: There are two bights, both on the west side of the point, that can be used as lunch stops in light weather or even for overnight in settled southeasterly breezes (a rare condition). The first, which is 0.3 miles south of the light, is in a slight indentation of the beach in front of the pond. The sand shelf here, about 10 feet deep, is a little wider because of the indentation and makes for easy anchoring. Be aware that the typical summer sea breeze is likely to freshen, creating a lee shore and a choppy surface. In a brisk northerly you will get too much sea coming around the point for comfortable anchorage.

Half a mile farther south is a larger indentation where the Galls start. The shore here provides better protection from the north and good protection through the east to southeast. The sandy shelf is broader here and makes for easy anchoring. This is the place to stop to go ashore and swim on the east facing the Atlantic beach.

DESCRIPTION: Great Point, Nantucket's most northerly extremity, is the southern inlet spit generated by the easterly flow of tide in and out of Nantucket Sound. The spit is about 2.9 miles long, extending northwesterly from the glacial moraine of Coskata. The end of

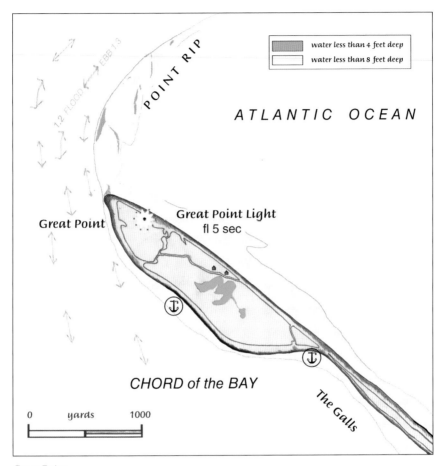

Great Point

the spit has been widened by tidal eddies that encircled a body of water to form a pond. It looks, on the chart, like a cattail. Most of my life this pond has opened southerly into the Sound, but today the currents have shifted sand to block its outlet. About half the original pond remains; the rest has turned to marsh.

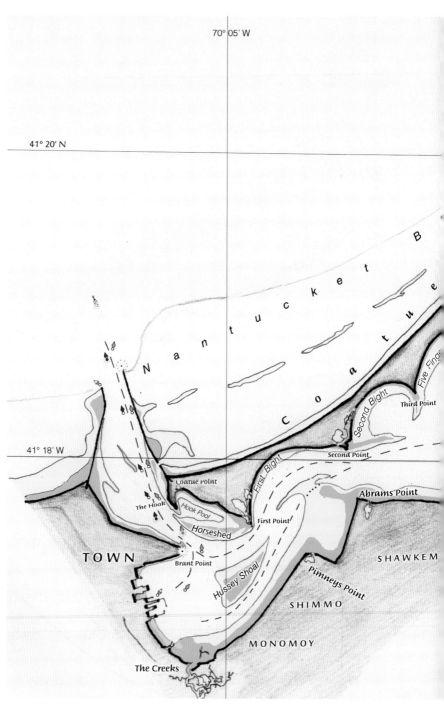

70° 05' W

41° 20' N

41° 18' W

N a n t u c k e t   B

N a n t u c k e t   C o a t u e

Five Finge

Third Point

Second Bight

Second Point

First Bight

Coatue Point

First Point

Abrams Point

The Hook

Hook Pool

Horseshed

SHAWKEM

TOWN

Brant Point

Hussey Shoal

Pimneys Point

SHIMMO

MONOMOY

The Creeks

Nantucket Harbor

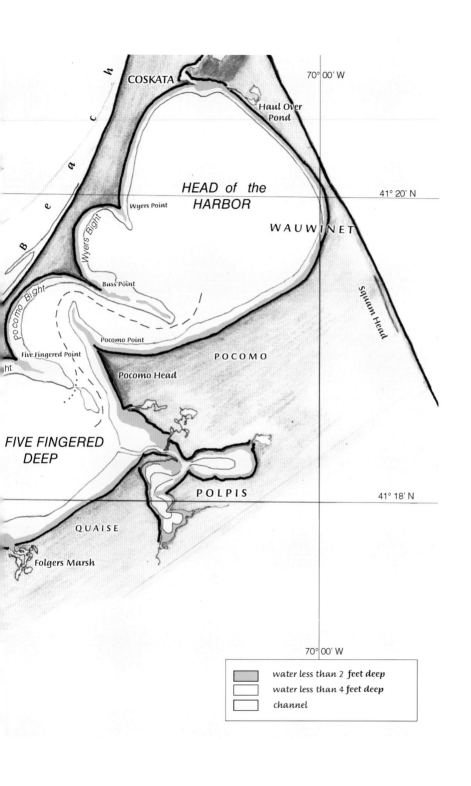

COSKATA

Haul Over
Pond

Beach

Wyers Bight

Wyers Point

HEAD of the
HARBOR

WAUWINET

Pocomo Bight

Bass Point

Squam Head

Pocomo Point

Five Fingered Point

POCOMO

ht

Pocomo Head

FIVE FINGERED
DEEP

POLPIS

QUAISE

Folgers Marsh

70° 00' W

41° 20' N

41° 18' N

70° 00' W

70° 00' W

	water less than 2 **feet deep**
	water less than 4 **feet deep**
	channel

The spit itself, connecting Great Point to Coskata, is called the Galls. Great Point, the head of the cattail, has doubled in size during my lifetime, while the Galls have been reduced in length about 30 percent. The Galls are higher now; what used to be pure sand is now a line of dunes topped with beach grass. This may be because of the benign winters the Island experienced between 1990 and 2010.

The spit is not as sturdy as it looks. Named the Galls for a reason—"Gall: a place rubbed bare; an unsound spot, fault or flaw," according to the *Oxford English Dictionary*—the spit is breached periodically by storm waves, and Great Point becomes an islet. Two weeks before the great Boston snowstorm of January 1978, a northeaster broke Great Point off from Nantucket, and it remained that way for the remainder of the winter. It happened again in the winter of 2012. But inlet spits are persistent, and the forces that created the Galls soon rebuilt the storm-caused damage.

Great Point carries a light mounted on a stone tower 71 feet above the sea. Before the age of steam this light was a very important mark for the coastal traffic traveling from Down East towards New York through Nantucket Sound. Getting into the sound from out at sea was not a trivial navigational feat. First built of wood in 1784, Great Point light burned in 1816. In 1817 a stone tower was erected that lasted until the currents undermined and felled it in 1984. The present tower is a replication of the 1817 tower. It was built with a broader foundation and in the center of the then point. The shore again is approaching the tower, but the sands are fickle, so who knows how long it will last.

Great Point does not stop at the water's edge. It extends under the surface as an arc of shoal called Point Rip that sweeps northeasterly for three miles to its outer end, which is marked by can "1." It is called "Rip" for a reason: the current runs across it strongly and can kick up a strong chop with unpredictable waves even in light weather. It is neither as clear nor as continuous as shown on the chart, however. There are spots as shallow as the "2"s indicated on the chart, and I have seen breaking waves there in an otherwise flat sea. But there are also openings running across the rip at least eight feet deep in places, and there is the usual inlet spit channel allowing currents to escape to the south just off the tip of the point. It is an interesting area and can be explored by small boat, but don't blame me if your vessel is stranded on a bar or capsized. Shoals and rogue waves are out here!

A sail to Great Point makes a fun outing. I remember in the 1950s sailing to Great Point with the family in my father's Raven. We'd anchor near the opening of the pond. We'd go ashore and our elders would set up a picnic while we kids played in the sand dunes. Because the spit starts here, it is a walk of only 50 yards to the east-facing beach that looks out over the broad Atlantic. Our parents suggested that if we looked hard enough, we could see Spain![2]

The swimming is good here, deep clear water with no weed. The swell breaks at the water's edge, but there is no surf as the bottom falls off too fast. Back then the fishermen's jeeps came by, but not often enough to disrupt the beach. Years later, that is not the case. As four-wheel drives became commonplace the outer beach became a highway, not a place for the pedestrian or sedentary. Today there is an infestation of seals on the point, which is making it less satisfactory for fishermen. Perhaps Great Point will become once again a wild place mostly accessible to boatmen.

Besides the outer beach, there is also good swimming on the Sound side. And to explore, the pond with its marsh, the lighthouse, two private beach shacks, and the exquisite beauty of the point itself where the waters of the Atlantic mix, crash, and swirl with those of Nantucket Sound.

---

2. Years later, in Bayona, Spain, I encouraged my children to look really hard—maybe they could see Nantucket.

Coatue Beach

APPROACH: Coatue Beach is approached either by coming in a southerly direction from the Sound or by passing through the Cut in the East Jetty, from the Harbor. Coming in from the Sound west of Coskata, you cross Nantucket Bar with four or five feet of water until you reach the beach. The Bar stops at Coskata; east of there deep water comes right to the beach.

BOTTOM: Sand. Good holding all along the entirety of Coatue Beach.

CURRENTS: No appreciable current until you approach Great Point.

PROTECTION: The presence of Nantucket Bar and the curving beach's relationship to the prevailing southwest wind make for different conditions along the beach.

In easterly and southerly winds anchorage on the beach is always protected. With northeast and north winds it is only protected in close behind Great Point. It is all exposed in northwesterly winds. The winter northwesterlies are what create its smooth crescent shape.

In the typical summer westerlies and southwesterlies the situation is more complex. Starting at the East Jetty, the beach is in the lee. As you move down the beach the wind comes along the beach and eventually onshore. Wave action is broken a little behind Nantucket Bar. By the time you reach the Galls the wind is onshore and the landing rough. In spite of this, a large boat can anchor off the Galls in moderate weather so close in that it is an easy swim ashore.

DESCRIPTION: Coatue Beach runs from Coatue Point to Great Point in a six-mile arc of sand that is one of the most perfect beaches in the world. It includes the Sound shore of Coatue spit, the Sound shore of Coskata, and the Sound shore of the Galls. The contemporary government charts have dropped the appellation "beach" from Coatue and renamed the area near Coskata as "Coskata Beach," but it is all one beach.

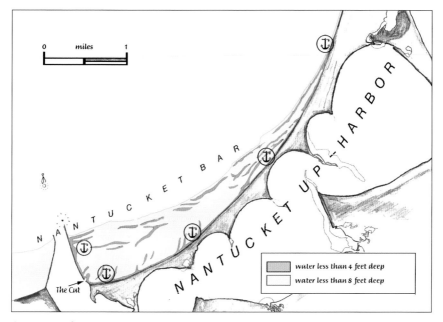

Coatue Beach

At Coskata Beach, Nantucket Bar terminates. The deep waters of the Sound, 50 feet or so, come right close to the beach, which rises from the depths at near 30 degrees, the angle of repose of wet sand. One light air night in June 1975, lost in dense fog, I sailed the yawl *Otais* onto this beach. The bowman was able to drop directly onto the sand without getting his feet wet. The steepness of the beach both told us where we were and made it easy to back off. We moved out 100 yards, anchored, and waited for the better visibility of dawn, as prudence would have had us do a little earlier.

East of East Jetty

APPROACH: Either go through the East Jetty cut and turn north till opposite can "5," across the jetty, or round the outer end of the jetty and come to the same spot from the northeast. Pick a spot with four or five feet of water. There are lumps here less than three feet deep.

BOTTOM: Sand. Good holding.

CURRENTS: The current always runs westerly here, onto the rocks, as much as three-quarters knot. Don't get too close.

PROTECTION: This spot has good protection from the typical south-westerly and none at all from a northeasterly. If the southwesterly shifts to the west it can get bumpy. The closer to Coatue you are the less swell, which will work its way around the end of the jetty.

DESCRIPTION: This is a good place to stop and await daylight to enter the harbor. In this case stay to the east well away from the jetty rocks. It is also a good place to watch the fireworks on the Fourth of July or Boston Pops Night.

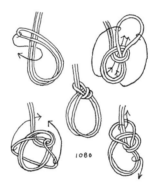

Bowline on the bight

8

Nantucket Harbor

Cutter

> Now we go to sea with not only electric lights, power winches,
> auxiliary motors and sewing machines, but even with radio,
> loran, echo sounders backed up with computers and satellites.
> We have changed the terms of the challenge of the sea, but we
> have not changed the sea itself nor ordered the weather.
>
> —Irving Johnson, *The* Peking *Battles Cape Horn*

NANTUCKET HARBOR was once known as the Great Harbor
when the town was moving from Capuam Pond to its present location in the early eighteenth century. It is formed by two sand structures, which accreted to the moraines left by the glacier. Haulover
Beach connected Coskata Bluff with Wauwinet to close off the
Atlantic in the east. And the barrier beach/inlet spit of Coatue
closed off most of Nantucket Sound to the north. A third structure,
the inlet spit now known as Brant Point, narrowed the entrance and
protected the inner harbor, while the outer harbor entrance was
protected from the Sound by Nantucket Bar.

Naturally, a bar shallow enough to keep waves out of the harbor was also shallow enough to keep substantial vessels out. The

channel across the Bar was nine feet at high water and doglegged across the Bar. The "Bug Lights," whose structures still exist behind the Cliffside Beach Club, were established as a range for one of the legs. It was a dangerous and uneconomical situation. Some ships were lost; all deep ships were inconvenienced.

In 1803 the islanders petitioned the federal government for help. There being no good response to their plea, in 1826, at their own expense, they unsuccessfully tried to dredge a channel across the Bar. The currents quickly filled it in. Meanwhile, they lightered loads into the harbor from ships anchored outside. Finally the islanders developed the "camels." *Camels* were moveable floating dry docks that, beyond the Bar, in deep water, would be submerged under a laden inbound ship. Then the camel would be pumped out, raising it and its load. Shoal drafted, it would be towed across the Bar into the deep water of the inner harbor where the process would be reversed—a lot of effort for the first and last miles of a voyage. This technique was used till the collapse of the whaling industry in the late 1840s.

The Jetties

Seventy-eight years after the original petition and thirty years after the last whale ship departed, the federal government sprang into action and started construction of the magnificent jetties that create today's grand entrance to Nantucket. Between 1881 and 1884 the western jetty was built 5,000 feet out over the Bar. But for the jetty to work to improve harbor access, it needed a companion on the east to focus the flow of tidal currents into a jet that would cut a channel across the Bar. Ten years after completion of the West Jetty, approval was given for the east one, all 7,000 feet of it. It was finally completed in 1901.

Immediately the focused currents began reshaping the shoals of Nantucket Bar. The depth across the Bar increased to 12 feet low water, and a clear channel was formed in a straight line. The jetties were placed so that the channel runs almost due north and south

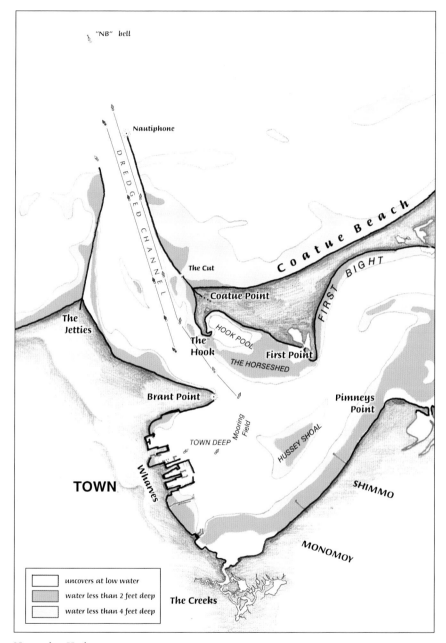

"NB" bell

Nautiphone

DREDGED CHANNEL

The Cut

C o a t u e   B e a c h

Coatue Point

FIRST BIGHT

The Jetties

HOOK POOL

The Hook

First Point

THE HORSESHED

Brant Point

Pimneys Point

Mooring Field

TOWN DEEP

HUSSEY SHOAL

TOWN

Wharves

SHIMMO

MONOMOY

	uncovers at low water
	water less than 2 feet deep
	water less than 4 feet deep

The Creeks

Nantucket Harbor

magnetic, 162/342 degrees true. Its direction allows a schooner to sail, in the typical southwester, the channel's length, close hauled, and round Brant Point without having to tack. As the exact point of crossing the Bar was optional, I believe it safe to assume that the designers well understood sail and chose it intentionally.

In the years 1970 to 1990 Bob Douglas of Vineyard Haven would bring his magnificent topsail schooner, *Shenandoah,* in under full sail (square topsails and all), round up around Brant Point, back his topsails in front of Old North Wharf, and drop his anchor. Once I had the thrill of sailing by *Shenandoah* in my 12-foot Tech dinghy as she came by past nun "6," everything flying, at about 12 knots, hissing along. I was to leeward of her, and though she changed my wind, she did not blanket me or leave me flapping on the other tack as the iron ferry would. Her wake even at 12 knots was not difficult. What a vessel! *Shenandoah* has no engine. Her entrance to Nantucket is similar to what some of the handier whale ships might have done—if the jetties had been built in their time.

The Steamer Channel

Today the Steamer Channel, as it is known locally, from its original use by the steam ferry boats, has a controlling depth of 11.4 feet. The mouth of the jetty opening is all deep water with the exception of a 7-foot shoal extending perpendicular from tippy end of the West Jetty rocks to about one-third of the way to the line of red nuns. At its very end, the West Jetty runs invisible below the surface for about 50 yards, but there is a white can marking safe clearance from the last rocks. On the western side of the channel most yachts can sail well wide of the line of red nuns until they come to nun "6," which should be honored. There is a shallow bar running from near nun "6" about halfway to the West Jetty parallel to the Brant Point (Hulbert Avenue) shore. I learned about this shoal at age eight when my mother helmed Dad's Raven into it and bent the centerboard. In my family it is known as Lizzie Shoal, but that name has yet to be confirmed by the U.S. Board of Geographic Names—the shoal is unnamed on the chart.

On the east side there is deep water, 15 to 20 feet right along the rocks, although the water near the rocks is usually encumbered with lobster pot buoys and their pendants. You can sail very close to the rocks, inside the line of pot buoys, if you wish, both because the water is deep and because the tidal current always, both ebb and flood, pushes you away from the rocks. But when you reach the bend in the jetty between cans "5" and "7," leave the rocks, continue straight, and reenter the channel at can "7." The water becomes very shallow around the opening through the jetty called the Cut.

The Cut

Originally the East Jetty was built as a submerged jetty with marker piles of rock every 200 yards. The top just poked above water at low tide. Because the submerged jetty did not create enough current to keep the channel scoured to the desired depth, it was raised in 1962 so that the top is just above water at high tide. At the same time, an opening was made through the jetty 500 yards from the then end of Coatue Point. This cut is a shortcut for small craft on their way to Great Point and beyond.

Although the Cut is 25 feet deep as it passes through the jetty, tidal inlet fans on either side restrict passage to 3 feet.

The heightened jetty did indeed increase current flow, and the channel has needed minimal dredging since. The increased flow has effected large changes on both shores alongside the channel. On Coatue it has extended Coatue Point several hundred yards to the west and created the Hook, a new point and cove altogether. On the Brant Point shore it set the Hulbert Avenue shore in fluctuation and created several acres of new land at the Jetties Beach, where the West Jetty starts.

Today, more than 50 years later, the East Jetty is in poor repair and below designed height. It is scheduled to be repaired and heightened.

Nantucket inner harbor with Coatue and Great Point beyond. The Hook is clearly visible on Coatue and the Cut can be seen on the extreme left if you look closely. Photo © Garth Grimmer.

The Horseshed

After can "9" on the east side, the channel runs by the Horseshed. The Horseshed steeply banks up from the depths of the channel to very shoal depths. It is shallowest on its edge near the channel and deepens slightly as it runs back to Coatue. It is full of clams, and during season you can see people walking around on the Horseshed, sometimes in ankle-deep water, digging. At extreme low tides an arc of sand following the edge of the channel is exposed.

It takes its name from an actual horse shed that used to be on Coatue. The shed housed horses ridden in from Great Point by the lighthouse keepers traveling to and from town. They would leave their horses in the shed and continue across the harbor by boat.

The shoal starts just outside the line of channel cans. One evening at dusk I ran *Impala*, 22 tons and drawing almost eight feet, aground here in the confusion of leaving for a Bermuda race. But the bank is steep and made of sand, so we were able to get free merely by steering away from it back towards the channel. The Horseshed is more captivating of smaller boats that might run up on top of it.

Inner Harbor

To get to the inner harbor, turn away from the Horseshed westward around Brant Point Light. Here is a fine basin integrated with the town by a series of wharves. We have paintings of the wharves crowded with whale ships and later photos of anchored fishing schooners filling the basin. This is the cove that connected Nantucket Island to the far-flung world.

The inner harbor at Nantucket is well protected, but it has one serious fault. The deep water of the designated anchorage area has a very soft mud bottom and poor holding.

Part of the reason for the poor ground is that the current coming past Brant Point splits just before can "13," one branch continuing up harbor and the other going towards the docks. The north end of the anchorage is in the dead spot in between the two flows. During change of tide there are circular currents here. You will see, in calm weather, for a half-hour or so around low and high water, boats on adjacent moorings headed opposite directions. It is a place where light debris falls to the bottom and forms a mud the consistency of onion soup. Not good holding.

While today this area is not available for anchoring, being entirely taken up with moorings, that was not always the case. In the 1950s, on a busy summer weekend, four or five visiting yachts would be anchored here. If caught by a summer northeasterly gale, often a couple of these yachts would end up on the sandy shore of Monomoy. I can remember in August 1954 during Hurricane Carol, several beautiful yachts, including the spectacular black schooner *Mistress,* aground near the Easton Street bulkheads with five-foot waves breaking over them—a sad sight indeed, but none of the boats were lost.

It may be hard for today's visitor to believe, but in the 1950s the harbor was very quiet. One summer the New York Yacht Club came in with 11 boats. This was a very big deal and the harbor was considered full! In the 1950s we used what was called the general anchorage, which is today the mooring field, for small-boat racing. Even races for the Yankee One Designs, 30-foot keel boats, were started here, with our first mark being either can "13" or a private buoy to the south in front of what was then the boatyard and is now Great Harbor Yacht Club. Rather than today's constant flow of ferries and large yachts, with at times three of four using the channel simultaneously, there were just two ferries in the afternoon, one Steamer and one Hyline. The rest of the time, small sailboats had the area to themselves.

A story from the Rainbow fleet may explain the mood back then. It was a good-sized fleet, and we all knew each other. One August day we were racing in the harbor. I was sailing my grandmother's boat, *Shee Goes.* The wind was light from the northeast. We were sailing from the boatyard (now GHYC) and headed around Brant

Point to the jetties against the incoming tide. The fleet was bunching up trying to round the point when the steamer *Nobska* came in. *Nobska* blew her whistle at Brant Point and was accosted by a fleet of 20, or so, Rainbows—maximum age of the skippers, 16.

The steamer captain stopped *Nobska*, a steam-powered, single-screw 250-foot vessel drawing 12 feet dead in the water. She was drifting with the fast-flowing current, 50 yards from the lighthouse.

The Rainbows proceeded. Some boats, in the lead, managed to sail around *Nobska*'s stern and continue on their way. Some boats bore off and went the other way, close around the plumb bow towering 30 feet above. Some were a little way back, approaching the scene carefully. Several were shouting at the steamer, "Sail over Power!" including the skipper of *Lindy Hop*, who, shaking his fist at the bridge, ran smack into the side of *Nobska*. I can still hear the clang of his bow fitting hitting her steel plates square amidships.

Our sailing mistress called the race and had a little talking-to for us in the sail room upstairs at the yacht club. A few years later the International Maritime Organization got into the act and changed the rules for Avoiding Collision At Sea (SOLAS) so that vessels whose maneuverability is constrained by draft—surely a classification fitting *Nobska* at Brant Point—have right of way, even over sail-powered vessels such as Rainbows.

That was then. Today it is a brave mother who would allow her children to sail near the main channel into Nantucket, and it is a good sailing boat that will make headway through the tens of power boat wakes that disturb the water. Such sailing is better done up harbor away from the traffic, and today, the yacht club starts its races to the east of Second Point.

Currents—Ebb and Flow

Generally speaking, the current floods in from the west into Nantucket Harbor through the mouth of the jetties. It runs down the channel to Brant Point, where it splits at Hussey Shoal, one stream

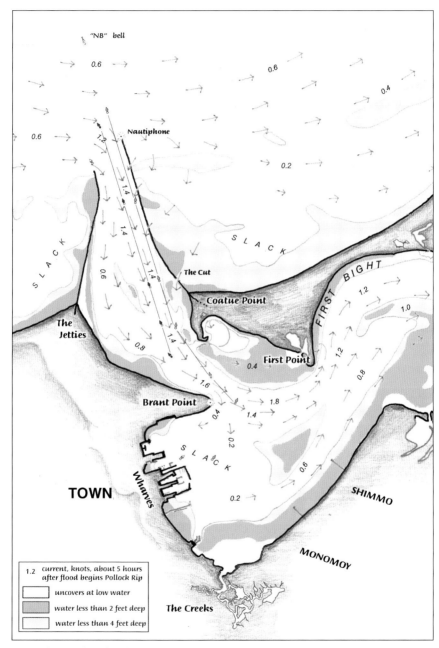

Nantucket Harbor, flooding tide

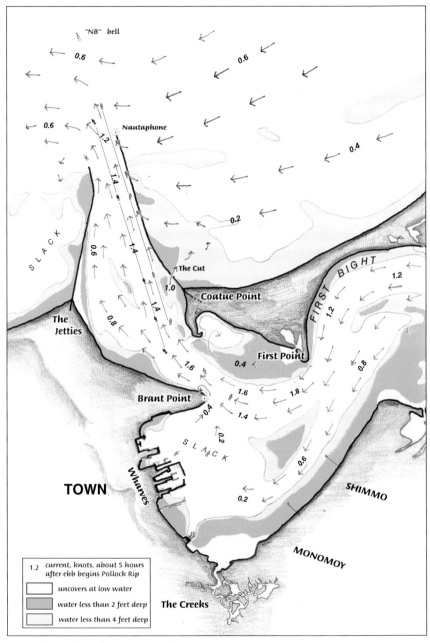

Nantucket Harbor, ebbing tide

running south into Town Deep and the other flowing to the east to make its way to Wauwinet. The south-going stream slows greatly 100 yards past Brant Point. It runs to and by Steamboat Wharf, to the Creeks, then curves to the northeast and runs up the back side of Hussey Shoal, eventually joining the other stream at Second Point.

The ebb—generally—reverses this flow. But there are a number of asymmetries between flood and ebb. Points of land which extend out into a stream usually have back eddies behind them. This causes the current to flow in one direction, both ebb and flood, in the small area of the back eddy. This condition is found on the north side of Brant Point and the east side of First Point.

On a bigger scale the same phenomenon happens on the East Jetty. There, during flood tide, the easterly current sweeps past the end of the jetty and back-eddies around to cross the rocks as a west-going current. During ebb flow, the general current is westerly and also runs across the rocks westerly. Consequently the East Jetty always has a current flowing through the rocks setting west, and if you sail close along the jetty, you will find it almost impossible to hit the rocks, as your boat is always being pushed away from them. This condition exists from the curve just past the Cut till abreast of the end of the West Jetty.

The points in Nantucket Harbor often have one shore that is parallel to current flow and the other perpendicular to it. These points have back eddies with only one direction of flow, which causes another asymmetry between ebb and flood. Brant Point has a strong back eddy on its east side in ebb flow but little on the south side in flood. First and Shimmo Points have the reverse, with the eddy occurring during the flood, but not the ebb.

It is generally true that the deeper waters have the fastest currents. Often channels are created by the scouring of the current. The exception to this rule is the deeps themselves, Town Deep, Five Fingered Deep, and Head of the Harbor. In the deeps, Bernoulli's principal holds sway, and the current slows down as the fixed amount of water flow is spread over a large area.

The Wharves

Around Brant Point is the historic waterfront. To understand the town of Nantucket, today, one needs to know about the magnificent set of interconnected wharves created for the whale industry by the islanders in the eighteenth century. The wharves were established first and are the reason for the town's existence.

In the seventeenth century, although the islanders farmed all over the island, their principal settlement was at Capuam Harbor on the North Shore.[1] But as the whale fishery developed, the islanders suffered the mariner's ever-pressing need for a harbor. They needed a landing place large and deep enough for their new, oceangoing ships. Capuam Harbor was inadequate for anything more than a beach boat.

The first land development in what is now the town area was the Wesco lots laid out between Steamboat Dock and Straight Wharf in 1678.[2] Not much happened with them for the next 40 years. Then, in 1717, two things happened: storms closed Capuam Harbor, turning it into a pond, and a lot of building activity started taking place on the Wesco lots and also on the Fish lots, recently created south of Main Street.

It is not clear exactly when the wharves were planned, nor when they were built. But we do have a 1723 plan showing the layout of warehouse lots, upland of North Wharf and Straight Wharf. On the plan the two wharves are labeled *"Old* North Wharf*"* and *"Old* Straight Wharf,"* implying they had been there for a while.

Although the history is vague, it is consistent with the facts we do have, that in the early eighteenth century, the first wharves were

---

1. A detailed history taken from town records is given in Starbuck, *The History of Nantucket.*

2. Lancaster, *The Architecture of Historic Nantucket,* 9–10.

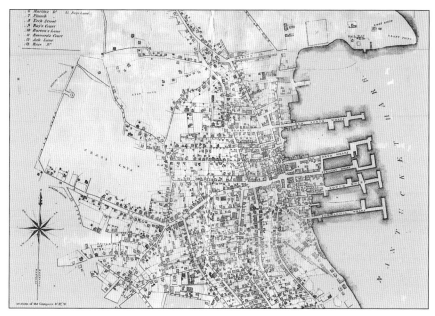

The 1834 Coffin map shows the historic wharves at their fullest development. Courtesy of the Nantucket Historical Association.

built. Ships started using them. Buildings were erected to service the ships. The ways down the wharves were extended inland and became the streets Broad, Cambridge, and Main. The activity caused people to move their dwellings closer to their work. Existing houses at Capuam were dismantled and moved, and new houses were built, on the residential Wesco and Fish lots. In a couple of years the town had moved from Capuam to its current location on the great harbor. The force effecting the move was the whalers' need for a good landing place to start and end their voyages.

Like many things in colonial Nantucket, the wharves were unorthodox at the time and of sophisticated design. Nantucket Harbor is subject to strong northeast winds, often of gale or storm force in winter. These winds blow down the five-mile length of the harbor from Wauwinet and create a considerable sea state, which the wharves had to mitigate.

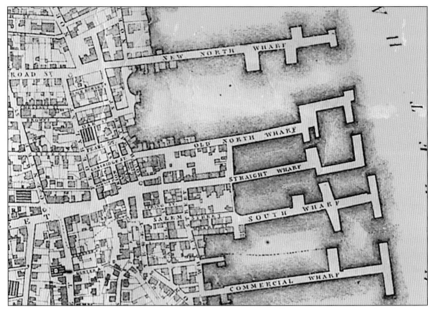

Detail from the Coffin map showing the intricate pattern of protected basins, a key feature of the 18th-century wharf design. Courtesy of the Nantucket Historical Association.

Of interest is the fact that storm waves in the harbor have a characteristic period that is resonant with the pitching period of smaller vessels. I lived for a few years aboard the 100-foot tug *Pegasus* in Nantucket Harbor. While the long waves of the ferry, entering or leaving the harbor, would make her roll on the calmest of nights, she was unmoved by wind wave action, even in strong storms. In contrast, 40-foot waterline *Impala* has broken loose three times during winter storms. Her pitching coincides with the waves, causing her to bounce so wildly that she snaps her dock lines.

The builders of the historic wharves were well aware of waves and their effects on docked vessels. Their design is shown on Coffin's map of 1834, drawn when the wharf system was fully developed. As you can see, the wharves as a group formed a barrier wall to the northeast. Narrow channels passed through gates in this barrier. The openings were about 40 feet wide, narrow enough that most

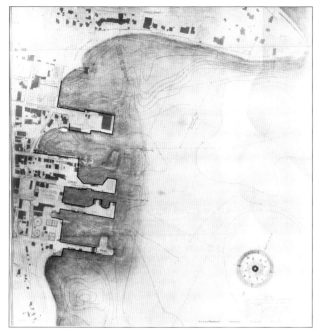

The wharves in 1938. They have not changed since the fire, excepting Steamboat Wharf has been filled in. The water's edge has been enhanced. Courtesy of the Nantucket Historical Association.

of the wave energy was reflected and the remainder was highly dispersed by diffraction. Then the channels passed through a second gate, where even on the stormiest day, waves would be nonexistent. The inner reaches of Easy Street Basin and the Boat Basin, the last remnants of the old design, benefit, today, from this feature of the old wharves.

The pattern begun with Straight and Old North Wharves was continued when South and Commercial Wharves were added to the complex. The steamboat dock, then called New North Wharf, was not so tightly integrated into the scheme. But even today, with only portions of Old North Wharf surviving, Easy Street Basin is remarkably quiet in a storm.

The great fire of 1846 burned the commercial town and the four southern wharves. The town never recovered financially and the wharves were not rebuilt. They had been constructed of large wood

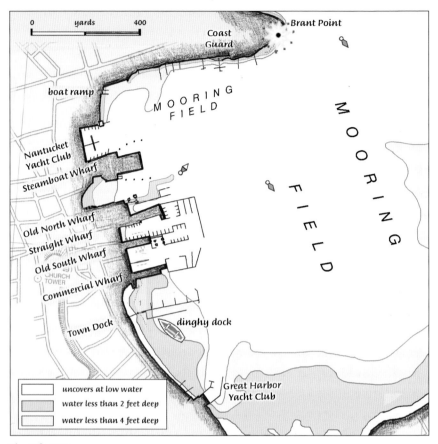

The Wharves

cribs, which were floated into place, then filled with stone to sink in their proper position. The timbers were logs, three or four feet in diameter, pegged together with four-inch-diameter wooden pins called trunnels. The fire burned the timber walls and let the fill collapse into the water.

New North Wharf was unburnt and Straight Wharf received some repair. The other wharves lay in ruins for over a hundred years. Cruising yachtsmen had to find their way in through the ruins to the few surviving berths or anchor out in the harbor.

Today the harbor looks quite different. The New North Wharf, now Steamboat Wharf, did not burn in the 1846 fire. Over the years it developed as the main ferry dock. It is now a state enterprise and very busy with large vessels connecting Nantucket's economy with the mainland. Yachts should beware the ferries and give them plenty of room to dock and maneuver.

North of Steamboat Wharf is Nantucket Yacht Club with many small-boat strings rigged between their bulkhead and launch floats. There are no visitor slips and few reciprocal privileges, the trouble being that because Nantucket is a resort, almost every one of the members also has a yacht club at home, and if the club extended reciprocal privileges, it would have few members in its own right!

North of the yacht club is the White Elephant Hotel with a few slips, mostly rented seasonally to sport fishermen. It is run in association with the Boat Basin. And out towards Brant Point is a series of small private residential docks.

Moving south from Steamboat Wharf, one comes to Old North Wharf. Old North Wharf burned badly in the fire, which left its east end destroyed. In the early 1900s, fish shanties were built on its upland ruins. They were used to repair small craft and to land fish and scallops. Over the years these have been gentrified into tiny summer residences. The ruins of the old wharf are mostly intact a foot below low water. Beware the yellow "NH" buoy off the east end of the wharf; it is there for a reason. There is no access to the town over Old North Wharf.

If a cruising yachtsman wishes to bring his boat to land, he had best try Nantucket Boat Basin. The Boat Basin is a contemporary marina that was built over the ruins of Straight, South, and Commercial Wharves in 1968. To maximize its capacity, the pattern of the historic wharves was abandoned in favor of narrow pile-supported docks and finger piers packed solid with 240 yacht slips.

The intent being summer usage, a wood pile palisade was erected to provide protection from easterly winds. It suffices, barring storm-force winds from the northeast. Fortunately storms are rare during summer. The Boat Basin has not been subjected to a northeasterly summer hurricane since it was constructed more than 45 years ago. When such a storm does arrive, it will be interesting to see what happens. Conditions are very rough during winter gales, but in winter the Basin is uncrowded and there is room for the boats to bounce around.

Behind the palisade the modern yachtsman will find all the amenities he expects, albeit at Nantucket prices. The Boat Basin is located on the remains of the wharves around which Nantucket Town was built, so it is well located and connected to the heart of the historic town. As Michelin would say, it is worth a trip.

Farther south, beyond the historic wharves, the town built a public pier in the 1980s. It provides many local craft slips and houses the Marine Department and the harbormaster. There is a dinghy landing for visitors.

At the extreme south end of the waterfront just to the north of the Creeks, a boatyard was built in the 1960s. In the early 2000s the boatyard was reduced in scope and moved away from the waterfront. On its site a second yacht club, the Great Harbor Yacht Club, was established. As part of the development, the boatyard's 20-ton straddle crane facility was repositioned behind the new clubhouse and continues in operation by Grey Lady Marine. There is no workspace, however, so any work requires an over-road haulage, limiting the utility of the facility. Great Harbor Yacht Club operates two docks with slips for their members and landing for their launch.

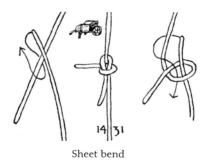

14 31

Sheet bend

9
Nantucket Upper Harbor

Catboat

> Like an inner sea protected by the barrier reef that breaks the thrust of the great ocean swells into millions of pearls, the lagoon is connected to the open sea by passes.
>
> Bernard Moitessier, *A Sea Vagabond's World*

KNOWN AS "Up Harbor," Nantucket's upper harbor is a five-mile stretch of water, bounded by sand, dune, and marsh. Its south shore is the north edge of the glacial moraine. Its north shore, separating it from Nantucket Sound, is the exquisite and unique scalloped sand spit of Coatue. The glacial moraine contains several tidal ponds: Coskata, Folger's, Shimmo, and the Creeks. Too large to be considered a pond but of similar structure is Polpis, two interlocked ponds in butterfly configuration connected to the harbor by a navigable channel. Up Harbor is a sailor's delight, with numerous landing places connected and organized by a channel from town to the hamlet of Wauwinet. It is analogous in many ways to Moitessier's precious lagoon.

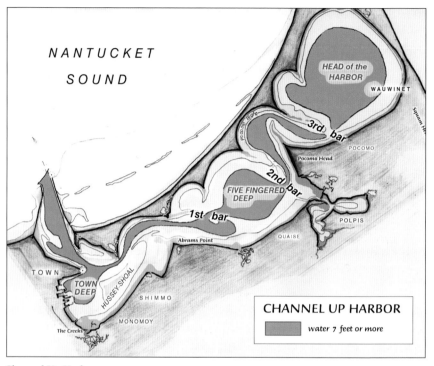

Channel Up Harbor

Channel Up Harbor

There is a good deep water channel leading from the town wharves to Wauwinet. It carries seven feet to Bass Point and five feet to Wauwinet. The channel consists of three deeps and two current-cut troughs connecting them. Two of the deeps, the one behind Brant Point in the inner harbor and the one at Head of the Harbor, are well known. The deep south of Five Fingered Point is less well known.

Let's have a look at the channel from the Sound to Wauwinet. Having come in from the deep water of the Sound in chapter 8, we arrive where the channel splits at Hussey Shoal. We followed the western branch that leads to the town wharves. To go up harbor we now take the easterly branch. The channel follows a serpentine path, not unlike a river, with the deepest water on the outside of the bends. It curves into First Bight and then sweeps past Second Point. It crosses its first bar (seven feet depth) south of Third Point and enters Five Fingered Deep.

From Five Fingered Deep, the channel, very narrow here if you need the full seven feet, crosses a short bar in front of Pocomo Head and again becomes riverine, sweeping into Pocomo Bight, looping around Pocomo Spit, and coming back to the southern shore east of Pocomo Head. The current is mostly spent by now, as the stream is close to its source, but there is enough, quite close to the shore, to cut a groove across the third bar (about five feet depth) and empty into the Head of the Harbor Deep.

Currents Up Harbor

The currents up harbor are fairly straightforward. They flood north-easterly and ebb southwesterly. Their range is three feet. Time of high water at Wauwinet is 1 hour after town, and you can pretty much prorate the difference along the way. Inside Polpis Harbor the constant is 45 minutes.

Where the channel is narrow and acting like a river, the current runs hard, exceeding one knot. At First, Second, Pocomo, and Bass Points the current runs strongly on the channel side of the points; while on the back sides, where the channel diverges away from the points, there is little. First Point has a strong back eddy on its eastern side during flood. Across the deeps, it slows to a quarter knot or less and disappears altogether in Head of the Harbor beyond Bass Point Bar. The ebb current from Head of the Harbor starts to flow fairly hard across Bass Point Bar. Once, I touched the bar on a falling tide and had to abandon my boat there to return the next morning at high water.

Six of the points of Coatue, a unique land form. Looking southwest towards Town. Bass Point and its bar, in the foreground, define Head of the Harbor. Photo © Garth Grimmer.

Coatue

Coatue forms Nantucket Harbor. Without it, there would be no harbor to speak of, and the Island would be far the less for it. Coatue spit, besides being the barrier protecting the waters of the harbor from the Sound, sits in the constant view of urban Nantucket—a reminder of the natural world that our industrial success has separated from us.

Partly barrier beach created by northwesterly winds of winter and partly inlet spit generated by tidal flow, Coatue is a five-mile sand spit running out from the morainal lump of Coskata. It creates, out of the wilder Nantucket Sound, five miles of protected waters. Its outer shore merges smoothly into the Galls and continues to Great Point, forming a classic crescent beach, seven miles long. Its south side is unique, at least in North America, scalloped into a series of five bights of similar size and shape.

As a land form, Coatue has attracted attention for a long time. Here is Nathaniel Shaler reporting on it to the U. S. Geological Survey in 1888:

> This remarkable district exhibits a number of very singular features. The most notable of these are Coatue Bay [Shaler's term for *Up Harbor*] and the sand beach which separates it from the sound on the north. Coatue Bay has the most puzzling configuration of bottom and of shores of any inlet on the North American coast. The bottom is divided into two great basins and a third one of lesser extent. In these basins the sea floor slopes gently from the shores to considerable depths, the two greater easternmost basins having about twenty feet of water at low tide, while the barrier between them has only about three feet of water upon it.
>
> The configuration of the shores is even more peculiar than that of the bottom. On the south, the boundary of the bay is quite irregular, being decidedly more indented than the general face of the island, for the evident reason that it has been protected by Coatue Beach from the action of strong waves. On the north shore of Coatue Bay the low dune-covered Coatue peninsular has six small crescent-shaped bays, of which five are very distinct in their outlines and of about the same size. Three bays are each a little less than a mile wide, and

the base of their curves is about two hundred yards from the line, which connects their promontories. From each promontory there extends for a distance of two hundred yards or more out into the bay a sandspit which is not delineated on the general map, but which, if presented, would add much to the peculiarity of their aspect. *** The cause of these peculiar projections is not plain. They are possibly due in some way to the action of tidal currents, which sweep up the bay with much speed and move the finely grained sand with considerable ease. From a superficial inspection it appears that the tidal waters are thrown into a series of whirlpools, which excavate the shore between these salients and accumulate the sand on the spits.[1]

Shaler makes the important point that each promontory continues as an underwater sandbar, out into the bay for a long way beyond the above-water point. These bars are an integral part of the fingers and affect the qualities of the bights between them. Each bight is waterscape of its own with its own special character. The bights themselves are not named. Because referring to them by their defining points is clumsy, I will give them names, starting at First Point and going northeasterly: "First," "Second," "Third," "Pocomo," and "Wyers" Bights.

Which brings us to the fact that the nomenclature of Coatue is hardly straightforward. The peninsula we call Coatue shows up on early maps labeled "Courtu Point" at its northwestern tip (1779), "Hanloetoe Point" on a map in 1801, and then from 1869 till 1965, "Coatue Beach," referencing its northern shore. On today's chart the "Beach" has been dropped and the entire spit has become "Coatue," which is the first time the peninsula itself is so named on nautical charts.

Today's charts show the six southeasterly projections named "First," "Second," "Third," "Five Fingered," "Bass," and "Wyers" Points. Fair enough to call these "points," if you like, and the names "First," "Second," and "Third" make sense if you are coming from town and counting as you go. "Bass" can be explained by good bass fishing that

---

1. Quoted in Starbuck, *The History of Nantucket,* 7.

was once there, and it is believed Wyers was named for a Mr. Wyer who had a place there. But "Five Fingered"? Where does this name come from? A. B. C. Whipple asks in his book *Vintage Nantucket*, "Where did it get that name? I could not find out."[2]

He has a good question. Five Fingered Point is the fourth point, not the fifth. And it certainly does not have, nor ever had in historical times, five fingers.

But perhaps we have an answer staring us in the face—the peninsula of Coatue itself is a five-fingered point, the "fingers" being the cusps of sand emanating from its south shore creating its unique and special form. On the early surviving charts the fingers are not named, nor is the peninsula itself. Only in the 1850s do the "fingers" become "points" and begin to acquire names. Perhaps, as they became "points" and were formally memorialized upon the chart, the label "Five Fingered Point" wandered from the middle of the whole spit to its middle finger, piloted, through a semantic fog, by mapmakers afar.

While logic might suggest that Coatue was named Five Fingered Point in the early days of the English, I know of no positive evidence. I find no document that has Coatue peninsula labeled as "Five Fingered Point." Mystery and doubt about the name remain.

The western end of Coatue, the shore facing Brant Point, has suffered similar indecision in nomenclature. Today's "First" point was unnamed on the chart of 1826, then became "Coatue" point in 1865, "Bogue" or "First" point in 1889, "Coatue" point again in 1930, before being named First Point, for the second time, in 1969. The northwestern tip, where the jetty starts, was originally "Cortu" point, then was without name, then became "First" point (1930), and now is "Coatue Point," Coatue and First Points having had their names interchanged between 1930 and 1969.

The western extremity of Coatue was round up till the end of the nineteenth century. This changed with the construction of the East Jetty, from 1898 to 1901. The jetty changed the current flow, which

---

2. Whipple, *Vintage Nantucket*, 255.

began a process that transformed the rounded end into two sharp points, First Point to the south and Coatue Point to the north where the jetty rocks begin. Finally, in 1963, the East Jetty was raised, causing a new flow that has generated between Coatue and First Points a seventh finger, now referred to locally as "the Hook."

Once we have the names straight, Coatue with its unusual shape and many concavities provides anchorages of all sorts. Here is a survey of them, starting at Coatue Point, continuing to Coskata, and then, leaving Coatue, moving around the harbor and back to the Creeks in town.

Front Face of Coatue

The front face of Coatue has been in a rapid state of flux for the past 30 years. In the 1960s it had a straight shore from Coatue Point to

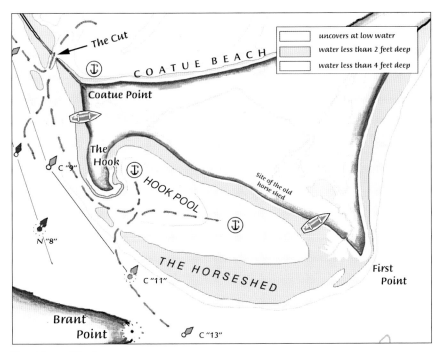

Front face of Coatue

First Point with a shallow channel just offshore running inside the Horseshed. At its west end was a fishing hole about 18 feet deep. The hole is shallower today, incorporated in Hook Pool. Raising the jetty in 1963 has resulted in quite different topography today. The Hook extends out onto the Horseshed, almost infringing on the channel. The delta fan of First Point Pond has extended to meet the Horseshed and cut off the inshore channel. And the Hook has made a nice new cove suitable for anchoring.

Coatue Point East

APPROACH: Go through the Cut and turn immediately south to anchor just off the beach in 6 feet. Access through the Cut is controlled by the bar on the harbor side at about 3 feet. Deeper boats can still reach here by going out around the nautiphone and approaching from the northeast—sail well east of the jetty and be careful making your way over the outer bar, which in places is only 4.5 feet deep.

BOTTOM: Clear sand bottom. Good holding.

CURRENTS: All the current rushes in and out of the Cut and leaves a quiet pocket here.

PROTECTION: Very protected in the normal summer southwester. However, this beach becomes a lee shore with winds from the northwest through northeast. In those conditions it is uncomfortable, and you might be happier on the west side of the Cut.

DESCRIPTION: Coatue Point is where the East Jetty meets Coatue spit. It has grown to the northwest about 2,000 feet since the jetty was completed in 1901, as the longshore current brings in sand that sticks in the rocks. The jetty rocks separate busy Nantucket Harbor from this quiet backwater of the Sound. Ironically, in the usual southwest wind, the Sound side is calm and quiet, while the harbor side is choppy and noisy from boat traffic. Here, wild Nantucket starts only half a mile from town. A seven-mile crescent beach starts here and runs to the tip of Great Point. Sitting here, with your back to Nantucket Town, the only structure in sight is Great Point Light, six miles across the water.

A little inland towards the overblown rocks is the wreck of a schooner that we kids used to play on during picnics on Coatue Point. It is a structure of 12-by-12s held together by 1-inch iron spikes. It could well be the remains of the *Ferguson,* which wrecked here December 16, 1904.[3] And it may be entirely covered by the sands now; I have not seen it for a while.

Coatue Point West

APPROACH: Stop short of the Cut and pull in towards the beach.

BOTTOM: Clear sand bottom. Good holding.

CURRENTS: There is a strong longshore current and no real anchorage.

PROTECTION: Basically exposed in all but easterly winds. This shore is subject to breaking waves from the ferry wakes and chop from the many speedboats using the main channel out of the harbor. The stop is suitable only for small boats that can be pulled up on the beach out of reach of the wakes. Larger boats should go to the east side of the Cut if the wind is in the south or to the Hook if the wind is northerly.

The Hook

APPROACH: Come in on a northeasterly course from the channel, perpendicular to the face of Coatue. Clear the end of the Hook by a little and come to rest in a hole about six feet deep. The approach carries only three feet at low water.

BOTTOM: Weed and soft sand. Moderate holding.

CURRENTS: Only a mild spinner, which keeps the pool from filling in.

PROTECTION: Good, except from the south, a rare wind in Nantucket.

---

3. Stackpole, *Life Saving—Nantucket,* 248–251.

DESCRIPTION: The Hook is a new cove created by the currents since the East Jetty was raised in 1963. The purpose of raising the jetty was to create a stronger current in the channel, and the Hook is an unintended side effect. Originally the East Jetty was a submerged one; the top just emerged at low water. The original configuration saved money and worked to cut a channel through the Nantucket Bar, but the channel needed dredging periodically because there was not quite enough current to maintain it. Raising the jetty increased the current, which now keeps the channel deep; it also is changing Coatue's shoreline.

The Hook is moving southeast and Coatue Point is growing northwest. The remnant of an earlier cove, first cut off to become a pond, has now filled and remains as low wet area. The Hook is also moving west towards the Steamer Channel. It leaves only a little room between its shore and the edge of the channel.

First Point West

APPROACH: Shoal boats can make their way across the Horseshed directly from the southwest. Deeper boats come from Hook Deep to the west and venture as far as the shoaling water will allow.

BOTTOM: Sand. Good holding.

CURRENTS: Little current.

PROTECTION: Good protection at low tide from all directions. Can be exposed to southwesters at high tide.

DESCRIPTION: This landing to the west of First Point is interesting mostly for the complex and extensive pond which enters the harbor here. The pond is full of life and is a good introduction to the sand dunes and marshes of Coatue. The tidal flow in and out of the pond has made a large fan out onto the Horseshed, cutting off the channel which in earlier days ran all the way to Coatue Point. Today the water west of First Point is extremely shallow—wading grounds at low tide. One often sees shellfishermen walking the bottom there.

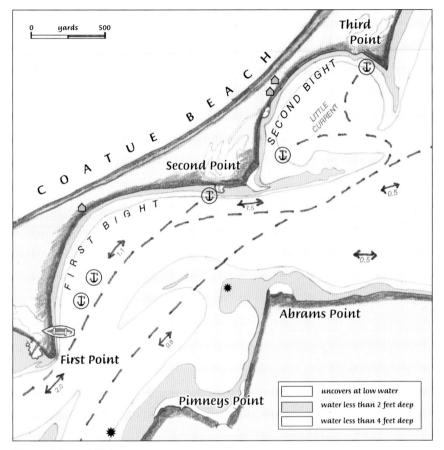

First and Second Bights

First and Second Bights

The shore of First Bight is a narrow sand beach backed by scrub, or "puckerbrush" in local parlance, all the way to Second Point.[4] The deep water channel follows the shore, about 75 yards off. There are two

---

4. Whipple, in his *Vintage Nantucket,* chapter 12, discusses the flora and fauna of Coatue at some length.

seasonal shacks near the middle of the bight. This channel is scoured by the current which sweeps into the bight on its way up harbor.

First Point East

APPROACH: Coming from town, pass the point by 100 yards and then turn in towards the beach as close as your draft will allow. Come back closer to the point, stop short of the foul area 40 yards from the end, and anchor or beach your boat there. The west side of the point is too shallow for anything but a kayak. At low tide you will walk your kayak.

BOTTOM: Sand with some weed. Good holding.

CURRENTS: The outgoing current runs hard here, 1.5 knots, especially if you are not close in. However, on a flood tide there is a back eddy that is much gentler. In close to the point, the current always runs south.

PROTECTION: Good protection from the usual southwesterly.

DESCRIPTION: First Point has also been strongly affected by the construction of the jetties. In colonial times the end of Coatue was rounded with a small corner on the south. A chart in 1889 shows an engineering structure extending from and sharpening the point. The chart of 1930 shows both Coatue and First Points (the names are interchanged!) well developed, with the pond opening to the east into First Bight. Finally the 1959 chart shows the face of Coatue flat (pre-Hook days), the pond opening to the west of the point, and the names as they are today.

Second Point

APPROACH: Second Point is approached from the south, and the best landing is made on its southwest side. If you desire to get into the east side, you must clear the long sandbar (the underwater extension of the point underwater) by sailing two-thirds of the way to Third Point, heading into Second Bight, and then returning on the north side of the bar. Having done so you can find very quiet anchorage 100 yards from the point in about 2.5 feet.

BOTTOM: Sand and weed to the west, sand east. Good holding once the anchor penetrates the weed.

CURRENTS: Strong current on west side, easterly with the flood and westerly with the ebb. Little current north of the point.

PROTECTION: West side is exposed in southwesterly, protected in a northerly or an easterly. East side is protected from the southwester, and of course from the north. Even in a southeasterly it gets a lot of protection from the shoals extending out from Second and Third Points.

DESCRIPTION: Second Point is beyond the reach of town. Here you are beginning to be "Up Harbor." The smaller classes race here and there is some speedboat traffic in the channel, but this is the beginning of four miles of quiet, idyllic waters mostly used by sailboats.

Second Point is developing a double point, with a little cove at the end. A long bar runs out from the point deepening very gradually, and the sandbar finally drops off after 650 yards. This is a favorite swimming place for children. Even a toddler can sit in the water of the bar and feel the water go by.

All the fingers excepting Wyers have a pond in their tip. Second Point's is a fairly extensive one that enters the harbor through a winding creek on the west side of the point.

Third Point

APPROACH: The bar off Third Point runs due south. The bar extending from Second Point runs east. By sailing east from Second Point about half a mile and then turning north, you will come into the bight and may choose to head into Third Point or backtrack to come into the east side of Second. If you have avoided the two bars, the water depth is about four feet shoaling as you get close to land. It is deeper at Third Point than Second.

BOTTOM: Sand and weed to the west, sand east. Good holding once the anchor penetrates the weed.

CURRENTS: There is little current in Second Bight, as the stream flows south of the Second Point Bar and dissipates in Five Fingered

Deep. Notice that the bar from Second Point runs easterly and the one from Third Point runs southerly. Little current penetrates Second Bight between them.

PROTECTION: The entire bight is relatively protected by the two bars, quite different from First Bight, which is exposed to east through south winds.

DESCRIPTION: Second Bight is off the beaten track. The two bars extending from Second and Third Points separate it from the channel carrying the traffic up harbor and also keep out the racing sailboats. It is a good place from which to explore Coatue by foot. There are two privately owned shacks mid-bight, and there are two ponds that exit into the harbor, one just west of Third Point and one east of Second Point near the middle of the bight.

The swimming is good at Third Point, though the beach is narrow.

Third and Pocomo Bights

Third Bight joins with Five Fingered Deep to form a large basin in the upper harbor, lacking both tidal currents and obstructions. A circle almost a mile in diameter can be inscribed within the six-foot depth contour. The Nantucket Yacht Club began making use of this recently by moving the small class racing from First Bight to Third. The strong currents and shallows of First Bight made the racing interesting, but complicated. Being unobstructed, there is little shelter in Third Bight.

Interestingly, at Third Bight's apex, Coatue is wide, perhaps because no current sweeps its shore to eat away the land. From beach to beach it measures about 580 feet—a distance exceeded only by the 1,010 feet across upper Coatue at Head of the Harbor.

Pocomo Bight, in contrast, is dominated by the current that sweeps the bight like a river going around a bend. It has built up extreme bars extending from Pocomo and Bass Points, and it has scoured a channel deep and close to Bass Point. The bars direct the movement of both boats and water and provide some shelter for landings at Pocomo and Bass Points.

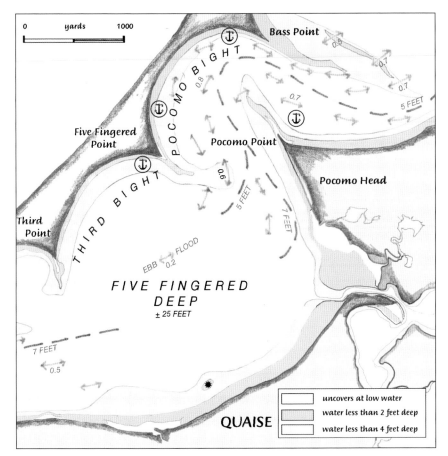

Third and Pocomo Bights

Coatue is at its thinnest at the apex of Pocomo Bight. From the harbor beach a walker may reach the Sound by crossing only 150 feet of scrub.

Five Fingered Point

APPROACH: Pass Third Point and approach from the south. Third Bight is open, without hazards or shoal water as you approach the land. It is shallower on the Third Point (west) side. Anchor to the west side of the point in five feet of water. Alternatively you can follow the main channel past Pocomo and come in from the east to the east side of the point and anchor in four feet.

BOTTOM: Sand. Good holding.

CURRENTS: There is little current on the west side of the point. There is current running along the east side of the point as the current sweeps through Pocomo Bight.

PROTECTION: Both sides of the point are open and exposed to southerly winds. Both anchorages are suitable for light winds and northerlies.

DESCRIPTION: Five Fingered Point has its fabulous name, which, as discussed earlier, was, I believe, acquired by default from the entire Coatue spit. Coatue, before construction of the jetties, was itself a five fingered point.

Five Fingered Point defines the east end of the middle section of Up Harbor, and Third Bight forms the northwest side of a circular basin, Five Fingered Deep, about a mile and a quarter in diameter. The basin is clear of shoals and has some of the deepest depths in the entirety of the harbor.

While it does not have the protection found between Second and Third Points, it is a great, beautiful bay that sees little activity. Stopping there, you are likely to have it all to yourself.

Bass Point

APPROACH: The west side of Bass Point, indeed anywhere along Pocomo Bight is approached by leaving the channel and sailing into the land more or less perpendicular to the shore, west to Five Fingered Point, northeast to Bass Point. There are no hazards and the water stays deep till you are near the shore. Just west of Bass Point there is anchorage in nine feet. The east side of Bass Point must be approached after rounding Bass Bar far to the south. This may be worth doing (see the following section on Wyers Bight).

BOTTOM: Sand. Good holding.

CURRENTS: The current is strong in Pocomo Bight, but it is not as strong as at First and Second Points because we are approaching Head of the Harbor; not that much water has to get out and in on each tide.

PROTECTION: Bass Point is generally protected from all directions although a little exposed to the south, a rare wind in Nantucket. The east side is protected except northeast through southeast.

DESCRIPTION: Bass Point Bar is the longest of all the points. On very low tides its extreme end comes out of water as an island. The point has a nice beach and the deeper water is on the west side. The west side is close to the channel up harbor, so there is traffic. To reach the east side one must go almost to Pocomo to get around the bar and then back to Coatue. It is less often visited. Windsurfers and kite boarders, working off the beach at Pocomo Point, sail the Bass Point waters extensively, but mostly on the west side.

Wyers Bight and Head of the Harbor

Wyers Bight between Wyers and Bass Points is very protected in the usual southwesterly. It has no current and deep water occurs near the shore, especially at the Wyers Point end. Because Bass Shoal forces all the traffic far to the south to clear its tip, there is little traffic; Wyers Bight is probably the most secluded spot up harbor.

Wyers Point

APPROACH: Wyers Point may be approached directly from the east or from the south after Bass Point and its bar have been cleared. This requires going almost all the way to the Pocomo shore.

BOTTOM: Sand. Good holding.

CURRENTS: Little current.

PROTECTION: Wyers Point is open northeast through south. Its bar runs a short distance out from the point, so there is protection from the east if you tuck in behind it close to shore. Coatue is

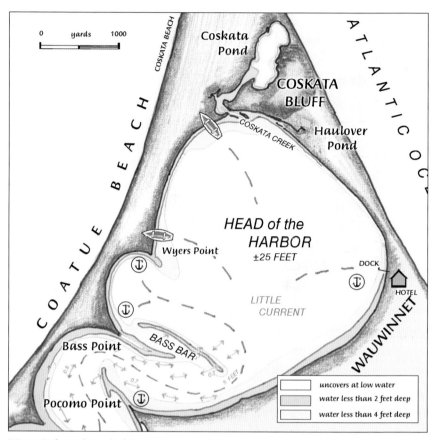

Wyers Bight and Head of the Harbor

running north here, so the typical southwesterly blows off the land rather than parallel to the beach. Bass Point, not far away, gives good protection from this direction.

DESCRIPTION: Rarely visited and well away from traffic, Wyers is a pleasant stop.

Head of the Harbor

At the end of the channel from town is Head of the Harbor, a landlocked basin about a mile and a half in diameter of deep, current-free water. Head of the Harbor is closed off from the sea by a narrow beach, called the Haulover, that joins Coskata Bluff with Nantucket Island at Wauwinet. In colonial times fishermen did indeed haul their small boats over the beach to launch them in the open ocean to the east. In the early twentieth century the ocean broke through Haulover, and there was for a while a channel through it to the sea. In time the cut closed up, leaving the vestigial pond and creek a few hundred yards south of Coskata Bluff.

In 1958 the eliminations for the Pan American Games and the U.S. Nationals were sailed in the then new Flying Dutchman Class in Head of the Harbor. About 60 boats from all over the country showed up to sail the Pan Ams in strong southwesterlies and for the Nationals in gentler winds. The boats were pulled up on the beach at Wauwinet, which was turned into a camp and sailboat shop for the week. Nantucket was chosen because we had just purchased a fleet of 31 boats, making ours the biggest fleet in the United States. We were far from the most experienced; the regatta left a strong impression on us locals.

The natural features that made Head of the Harbor good for those high-performance contests still make it one of the finest places in the world for small-boat sailing. Around its perimeter are a number of stopping places worthy of a picnic or an overnight.

Coskata and Coskata Pond

APPROACH: Continuing along Coatue past Wyers Point one comes to the end at Coskata Bluff. It is easily approached from all directions with no hazards. Anchor just west of the creek.

BOTTOM: Sand. Good holding.

CURRENTS: No current.

PROTECTION: Protection is only in the lee of the beach. Head of the Harbor is big enough that an onshore breeze will kick up a chop.

DESCRIPTION: Coskata is a bit of moraine about 30 feet high, covered with a dense tangle of puckerbrush. The longshore currents joined it with the Island as a whole and went on to build the Great Point and Coatue spits, which extend from Coskata to the northwest and southwest. In the process they enclosed Coskata Pond. At Coskata's eastern shore Nantucket Harbor ends and the great Atlantic begins.

The beach here is a traditional place for picnics and gatherings. I have seen as many as 10 boats anchored off the shore and 30 or 40 friends playing on the beach. The beginning of Coskata Creek is a wading adventure for children. Their braver elders, at high water, can take a 30-inch draft boat up the creek all the way into the pond. After the first 180-degree bend and the next 90-degree reverse bend, the shallow creek opens into the pond proper, which is quite deep water.

The pond and the bluff are mosquito infested. The beach is not.

Just to the east of Coskata Creek, south of the bluff, is Haulover Pond, which is the remains of the opening of the Haulover a hundred years ago. It is small and best explored on foot.

Wauwinet

APPROACH: Wauwinet lies at the end of the channel from Nantucket, at the southeast corner of Head of the Harbor, and is approached directly with no off-lying hazards. The bottom shelves slowly and one can anchor in three feet about a hundred yards from shore.

BOTTOM: Sand and weed. Good holding.

CURRENTS: No current.

PROTECTION: The southwest wind blows directly onshore with a long fetch from Pocomo. There is a good chop here if the wind has any strength. The dock and float are best approached from the north side. The water around the float and dock is shallow.

DESCRIPTION: South of Coskata in the extreme eastern reach of Nantucket Harbor lies the hamlet of Wauwinet. The hamlet became established in 1875 with the construction of the Wauwinet House, a beachside hotel. The hotel became a social focus. The owners developed lots, which they sold to those customers who enjoyed their summer stays enough to wish a more permanent presence. The hotel had its ups and downs through the twentieth century and finally, in a state of decay, was bought by the current owners, who have developed it into a fancy resort.

Although the best way to get to the Wauwinet House in the early days was by catboat from the town docks in Nantucket, the hotel was never, and still is not, oriented to boats or boating recreation. It is, however, the only commercial spot up harbor, and it has a dock— albeit a poor one—servicing the hotel and its restaurant. The hotel runs a small boat to and from town.

Pocomo Head and Point

APPROACH: Coming from town, follow the main channel beyond Pocomo to Bass Point and then veer back to the southeast to come in behind the point. Drop anchor 100 yards off the beach in 4 feet of water. Coming from Wauwinet, approach through the neck of deep water along the southern shore of Head of the Harbor to miss the extremely long bar extending out from Bass Point.

BOTTOM: Sand and weed. Good holding.

CURRENTS: Moderate current.

PROTECTION: Good protection from southwesterly and moderate protection from northeasterlies. In northerlies you will probably be better off on the Coatue side of the harbor.

DESCRIPTION: The high morainal bluff of Pocomo Head is very conspicuous from Nantucket Town. The winds have eroded its face to a straight, smooth, steep-faced cut that shows up as white under bright afternoon sunlight.

At its north end, Pocomo Point and its sand spit project far into Pocomo Bight. The spit is formed by and guides the tidal currents flowing into and out of Head of the Harbor.

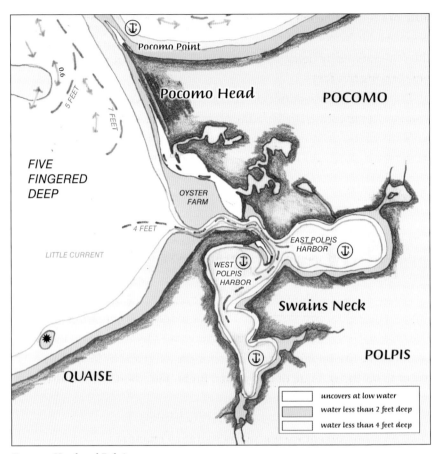

Pocomo Head and Polpis

The Point, connected to the general road system by Pocomo Road, is a favorite launching spot for wind and kite surfers and provides vehicular access to Up Harbor. East of the Point is a good anchorage protected by the underwater bar from the usual summer southwesterly.

Polpis

Butterfly-shaped Polpis Harbor is different in character from any other part of Nantucket Harbor. It is surrounded by marsh with little of the sand beach that dominates the other shores, and yet it is quite a bit bigger than the other tidal ponds. It also differs from the other ponds by being connected to the main harbor by a channel carrying five feet.

The harbor consists of two lobes, East and West Polpis. East Polpis, after entering the winding channel, is a six-foot-deep basin with a small beach at the end. West Polpis is more riverine. It winds, branches, and ends in rivulets of marsh.

East Polpis

APPROACH: The beginning of the entrance channel is marked with a town buoy. From there the channel runs straight into the beach to the west of the opening. Leave the second nun to the port! Turn east, running close along the shore, and then turn south into the opening. This is a tidal inlet structure and, as is typical, the deep water is along the beach; the entrance is blocked by the usual fan. The channel across the fan has been improved by dredging. Once you are into the opening, treat the channel as a river—the deeper water is on the outside of the bends. Right, left, then a right turn into the east lobe of Polpis Harbor.

BOTTOM: Sand, mud, and weed. Soft, okay holding.

CURRENTS: No current except in the entrance channel.

PROTECTION: Landlocked and small; the protection is complete.

DESCRIPTION: East Polpis is an oval-shaped pond. Many boats are moored here and there is room for a few visitors. There are often odd and interesting craft here because it is a perfect haven for pocket cruisers and other unusual craft which might not feel at home in the openness of the main harbor. Nantucket Community Sailing runs part of its sailing school off the beach at the extremity of East Polpis. It has a shed with lots of boats and gear there.

There is road access at the end of the harbor with a dirt road back to the paved Wauwinet Road. The rest of the water's edge belongs to private estates and is generally marshy and of poor access.

West Polpis

APPROACH: After coming to the old and somewhat derelict wooden bulkhead structure on the west side of the entrance channel, rather than turning east into East Polpis, turn 90 degrees to the southwest, passing to the south of the structure into West Polpis. Continue straight till the southeastern branch opens up, and then turn southeast into it. Stay pretty much in the middle where there is about five feet of water. After passing Swains Neck, the channel bifurcates, one branch continuing to the southwest and the other running to the northeast. Both end in marshes controlled by private estates. The docks are private. The water is public—and as beautiful as anywhere on earth.

BOTTOM: Mud and weed. Soft, fair holding.

CURRENTS: No current.

PROTECTION: Landlocked and small; the protection is complete.

From Polpis to the Creeks

The southern shore of Nantucket Harbor from Polpis back towards town is the back side of the glacial moraine. It is relatively high, with short stony beaches and a muddy sand bottom. This stretch receives little of the wave action that sorts out the glacial material and renders Nantucket's outer beaches such fine sand. The glacier has also left few erratics—large, potentially hazardous boulders—along this shore and out in the harbor bottom.

There is a secondary channel along this shore, running up harbor from town to Five Fingered Deep. The main channel current, as you remember, divides on the north side of Hussey Shoal. One branch goes up harbor along the Coatue shore and the other turns south towards the Creeks. This second stream curves past the creeks, turning northeasterly and streams south of Hussey Shoal along the Monomoy, Shimmo, Shawkemo shores to rejoin the other stream at Abrams Point. Along the Monomoy shore the current scours a channel about eight feet deep. From Pimneys to Abrams Point it is three or four feet deep and moves away from shore towards the middle ground between Pimneys and First Bight. Beware the erratic 200 yards west of Abrams Point. At extreme low water it is exposed, and sometimes it is marked with an informal buoy. The current in this secondary channel is significant, but not as strong as in the primary channel on the Coatue side.

There are four tidal inlet systems along this three miles of shore: Folger's Marsh at Quaise, Shawkemo Pond at Abrams Point, Shimmo Creek at Pimneys Point, and the Creeks just west of Monomoy. Folger's Marsh, Shawkemo Pond, and Shimmo Creek are navigable only by kayak. Each is a tidal inlet with a fan protruding into the harbor. Once across the fans, very shoal draft boats can enter the deeper waters of their labyrinthine channels. Their details are beyond the scope of this book. But the Creeks are another matter.

The Creeks

APPROACH: The Creeks are entered just to the east of Great Harbor Yacht Club over the bar made by the tidal fan at their outlet. The deeper channel (not very deep—a normal boat will need high water to enter the Creeks) is serpentine. The entrance is a little to the east of the opening; sail south- and southwest till you come to the bar, then turn to port a little and sail in towards the beach at the eastern side of the opening. When you get there, turn west toward the narrow opening in the marsh. Cross the last of the bar staying close to the north bank, and you will be in.

BOTTOM: Sand, hard. An anchor will hold, but a boat will be blown in one direction by the wind and pulled in another by the current. Generally, the Creeks being so narrow, your boat will be lying against one bank or the other. Except in extraordinary circumstances, this is not a good place to stop.

CURRENTS: Strong ebb and flood currents.

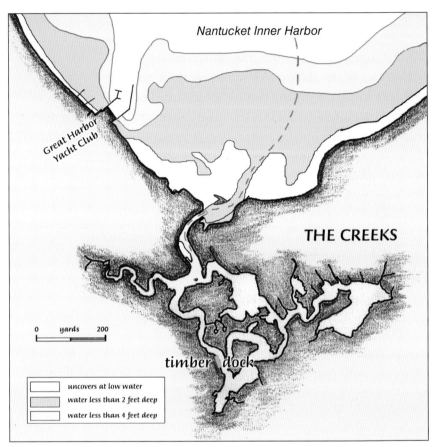

The Creeks

PROTECTION: Landlocked; the protection is complete.

DESCRIPTION: The Creeks, sometimes called the Monomoy Creeks, are the largest and most complex of the tidal systems in Nantucket Harbor. They form the southern bound of the town's waterfront. Once inside the Creeks, you will find yourself in a riverine-type system. The channels are deep with vertical banks dropping down to as much as six or eight feet. The banks are mud held together by marsh grass roots. The currents run strongly with the ebb and flood scouring the bottom and refreshing the waters, which are full of small life. Unlike a river, the channels double back on themselves forming islands and ambiguous spots where it is impossible to tell whether one is going upstrem or downstream.

Because of the difficulty in entering the Creeks at low water, it is best to plan a cruise into the Creeks for high tide. Although there are a couple of pools where one might pause, there are no real stopping places, so a cruise there is one of coming and going. There is a private landing stage, not far from the entrance.

The farthest reach of the Creeks is two-thirds of a mile from the entrance and involves 17 turns. The Creeks are labyrinthine and beautiful.

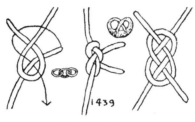

Carrick bend

10

The West End

Cat ketch

Have you ever lain timeless in a coracle-skiff with your nose half an inch above the mirror surface, drifting silently with the stream, your eyes probing down into the quivering green cool littoral below? You haven't? A pity. It's magic.

—Ken Duxbury, *Lugworm Island Hopping*

FEW MARINE AREAS are as beautiful as the west end of Nantucket. Comprising Eel Point, Smith Point, Madaket Harbor, and the islands of Tuckernuck and Muskeget, it is a region of shallow water, marsh, flats, and sand. Less developed than the rest of Nantucket, it is here that the natural beauties of the waterscape have their clearest expression.

The west end consists of three very different regions: the ocean-exposed south shore, the north side in lee of the islands, and Madaket Harbor, tucked in between.

Channels

Although most of the water flowing in and out of the Sound from the ocean runs north of the islands and reaches the sea through Muskeget Channel, there is a definite channel from Eel Point into Madaket Harbor and continuing on past Smith Point and out to the

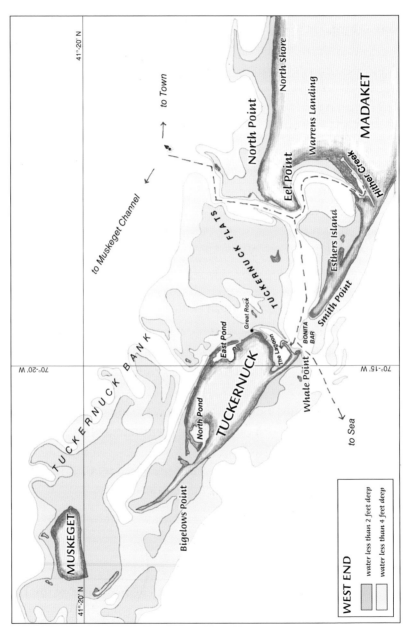

The West End

sea. This channel has a controlling depth of about seven feet, shallowest at the entrances, and a branch channel into Hither Creek with least depth of five feet.

The tidal currents flowing through the inlets between the islands deposit sand on the north shore as delta fans. Opposed by the smaller waves from the Sound, these fans consist of a maze of sandbars running along the north side of the islands about eight miles from Eel Point to beyond Muskeget. The moving sands have enclosed three ponds on Tuckernuck, two on the west end, one on the east.

There is no clear channel running to the sea between Tuckernuck and Muskeget. There are disconnected deeps separated by boomerang-shaped shallows that will leave all but the lightest draft vessels stranded.

Farther on, between Muskeget and Martha's Vineyard's Chappaquiddick, there are three passages. Two of these are difficult and rarely used: one close into Muskeget and one just to the west side of Muskeget Rock. The third channel is the well-marked Muskeget Channel, passing just west of Mutton Shoal. Leading to these channels, on the north side of Tuckernuck, is the deep east-west channel, at least 15 feet deep, running from the Eel Point bell to Mutton Shoal. It has a very narrow place, about a quarter-mile wide, at a point just north of Muskeget, but if you can navigate this constriction, it is a good passage and the fastest way from Nantucket to New York and points farther south or west.

There are a number of interesting landings and anchorages off these channels. I describe the principal ones.

North Shore

EEL POINT EAST

APPROACH: Turn due south about 0.4 miles before reaching the Eel Point bell. Watch for the very shallow water along the east side of

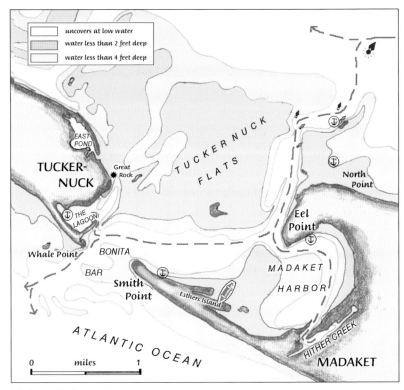

Madaket Harbor and approaches

the Madaket Channel. If you get into that, you are too far west. Sail towards the beach till you run out of water about 0.2 miles offshore.

BOTTOM: Sand. Good holding.

CURRENTS: There is moderate current here, westerly ebb, easterly flood.

PROTECTION: The protection is from the shoal water to the west and the land to the south. The anchorage is good, with winds from west through south to southeast, and best at low tide when the shoals give maximum effect.

DESCRIPTION: There is a protected anchorage from southwest winds just east of the knuckle, called by some North Point. This knuckle has been building on Eel Point for the past 50 years, having started when Hurricane Esther first cut through Smith Point in 1961. I spent a quiet night here on my first round-the-island cruise in 1975. I was sailing *Queen Jane,* a modified C&C Shark Class, a light displacement narrow fin keeler of 24 feet LOA.

EEL POINT DRY SHOALS

APPROACH: Turn south around the Eel Point bell and enter the Madaket Channel. On the east side near the first town channel mark you will come to the northernmost dry shoal. Anchor on the edge of the channel close to the shoal.

BOTTOM: Sand. Good holding.

CURRENTS: There is strong current here, southerly ebb, northerly flood.

PROTECTION: The protection is only from the shoal. This is a day-time, fair weather anchorage only, and the boat should be watched.

DESCRIPTION: For low tide only, there are one or more dry shoals north of Eel Point east of the Madaket Channel. They move around a bit both horizontally and vertically. Called "dry" shoals because they dry at low water, they are perfectly clean, being washed by the high tide every six hours. Being dry most the rest of the time, they do not accumulate mud or weeds. They are often covered with birds or seals. I remember an afternoon when, headed for Tucker-nuck, the dying breeze left us short of time. I anchored all 57 feet of glorious *Impala* here with her 8-foot draft, a swimming pool's length from the dry sand. We swam off the boat and used the little island as a base. It was the first place my three-year-old daughter was courageous enough to jump off the boat and into the sea.

Madaket Harbor

I spent several summers in my early youth on the beach of Madaket Harbor. My siblings, cousins, and I would play on the beach, limited on the south by the marsh of Jackson Point and on the north by the Warren Landing Creek. We had a child-sized skiff built by Herman

Minstrel, a local Madaketter, who had built the summer house we lived in. The house was called "Westward Ho" because of its location on the island and as an ironic reference to the American pioneers of whom we were quite conscious. It was close to the beach, and so integrated was our life with the shore that before entering this house we were encouraged to rinse the beach sand from our feet in a pan of water. We were paid a penny to do so. A tic list was kept by the door, and on an active day you could earn 10 cents.

My grandfather would take us sailing in his Town Class Sloop. He was a big man and the miniature skiff was much too small for him, so he would wade out into the water the 150 yards to where the boat was moored and climb aboard. We children could have done so as well, but we did not like the feel of the seaweed through which we had to walk. We were familiar with the scallop shells we found on the beach but were unaware of the live scallops living in the eel grass that covered the harbor bottom. After a westerly blow the grass tears away from the bottom and washes ashore to cover the beach.

Gramp would sail us as far as Smith Point, which was a long way for us children, and scary too, because it opened into the great Atlantic and had strong currents that could suck you out. Later we would sail ourselves in a Rainbow, being careful not to go much beyond the end of Eel Point. These centerboard boats were able to sail in 18 inches of water, so we could sail the entire basin, and, excepting a few fishing boats, we had the place to ourselves.

Before it was developed in the 1980s, the locals would retire to Madaket for the summer to avoid the seasonal rush in town. Today, Westward Ho is a parking lot, and for refuge, one must go to Tuckernuck, which has been a tougher "nuck" for developers to crack. Rather than Gramp's two sailboats, moored off Warren's Landing is a cluster of outboards and a few sailboats. Replacing the discarded and rotting catboats in the Hither Creek marsh, at the boatyard are several hundred antiseptic fiberglass runabouts.

But many things have stayed the same. The beach, the flats, the marsh, the creek, and the eel grass are still there. The fresh salt breeze still blows in direct off the Atlantic. After the rush of a summer afternoon the cruiser, anchored snugly in one of its corners, still has this serene and beautiful place to himself.

EEL POINT COVE

APPROACH: Follow the channel easterly around Eel Point and then ease north to the bight enclosed by the point itself. Seven foot of draft can be carried into the cove. Watch the water depth and get as far in as your draft will allow.

BOTTOM: Sand and weed. Good enough holding.

CURRENTS: Little current here.

PROTECTION: Protection from all wind directions, little current and no sea. This is a good anchorage.

DESCRIPTION: The bight between Eel and Smith Points is one of the most serene and beautiful in southern New England. It has everything but rocks and deep water: sand dunes, sandy beach, flats, marsh, pond, and creek. The bight is mostly shallow—two or three feet—but there is a distinct channel close around Eel Point and then following the shore to Hither Creek. To the north of the channel tucked in east-northeast of Eel Point is a cove with a deep water anchorage.

This south side of Eel Point is a marsh drained by mosquito ditches. The idea of the ditches is that since mosquito larvae need a stationary water surface to survive, by bringing tidal action to the marsh, the up and down will prevent mosquitoes from spawning. I am sure it works, but there are still some mosquitoes here.

There is a narrow sand beach along the marsh from the end point running about halfway to its base where it is interrupted by the ditching. To get farther towards Madaket proper you will have to wade.

HITHER CREEK

APPROACH: Continuing beyond Eel Point Cove, the channel shoals to 3 feet. It runs 200 yards off the beach past Warren's Landing—reputedly, and plausibly, the place where the English came ashore to purchase Nantucket from the Wampanoags—past Jackson Point into Hither Creek. The Creek runs northeast up to the boatyard, where it ends in marsh.

BOTTOM: Muddy.

CURRENTS: None.

PROTECTION: Entirely protected.

DESCRIPTION: Hither Creek is an entirely landlocked estuary, three-quarters of a mile long and a little over 100 yards wide, that holds the fishing fleet for the west end of Nantucket. There is no general anchorage, and if you need to ask where you are to stop, you cannot. At the end of the estuary is Madaket Marine, a general boatyard that caters to the outboard motor fleet and has dockage and fuel.

Halfway up the creek is the public pier, which is used as a pickup spot and has a boat launch ramp. Most of the heavy traffic to Tuckernuck passes over this pier named for the late Walter Barrett, who among many other things ran a ferry service to Tuckernuck from the pier.

Due to flukes in the writing and administration of Nantucket's zoning laws the only two commercial operations in Madaket are the boatyard and a restaurant called Milly's. This is too bad, because Madaket has everything else needed to be a proper village—loyal citizens, a secure harbor, and beautiful surrounds. Nonetheless, Milly's is there and is named for one of Madaket's most famous daughters, Mildred Jewett of the U.S. Coast Guard Auxiliary. Today Milly is a heroine of the past whom we can only admire. And while there is no doubt that her stern heroism was highly appreciated by mariners in distress, in the early 1950s, for me she was more of a troll terrorizing the bridge to the land of ice cream. Where was Billy Goat Gruff when you needed him?

South Shore

At the West End, the south shore suffers the impact of the ocean waves, constantly eroding the moraines and putting their sands in motion. The west winds also have an effect. At the end of Madaket's Massachusetts Avenue they will pile sand into 30-foot dunes and then remove them a few months later, depositing the sand elsewhere. The ocean tide enters Nantucket Sound between the islands, and its currents deposit the sand on the inlet spits of Smith Point, Whale Point, and Bigelows Point. Twice in recent years storms have breached Smiths Point to create and re-create Esthers Island. Currents running through the breaches strongly affect the shoals in Madeket Harbor and at Eel Point. When the breaches close, things tend to stabilize.

SMITH POINT

APPROACH: Follow the channel from Eel Point towards the Lagoon. Two-thirds of the way out from Madaket, head southerly in towards the shore and anchor a quarter-to-half mile before the point in eight feet of water. The bank between Hither Creek and Esthers is so shallow, the route to Esthers from Hither Creek goes via Eel Point.

BOTTOM: Sand. Good holding.

CURRENTS: There are strong currents around the end of the point as water rushes in from the sea over the Bonita Bar. Back from the point on the north side, the current floods east and ebbs west strongly along the beach. Except in strong breezes, your boat will generally lie to the current parallel to the beach.

PROTECTION: Well protected by the beach from east through south to northwesterly breezes. All but a strong northerly will be broken up by the shallows of Tuckernuck bank.

DESCRIPTION: The water north of Esthers is so shoal that there is no practical anchorage. A small boat can be drawn up on the beach here. Back when Esthers was an island, the eastern of the three houses here was supplied by a landing craft–style vessel which dropped its ramp directly on the beach.

Hither Creek, Madaket's inner harbor. The boatyard is visible at the upper end, and the bridge giving vehicular access to Smith Point is in the foreground. Off the picture, not shown in the foreground, is the tiny barrier dune that separates Hither Creek from the Atlantic. Photo © Garth Grimmer.

When Esthers is not an island (it is not at the time of this writing), Smith Point is the western tip of Nantucket. It is a spit formed by longshore currents and tidal inlet effect between Nantucket and Tuckernuck. There is a nice anchorage back a little from the end of the point. The point is always changing. It reaches over to Tuckernuck and then is cut back. I have seen it with ponds at the end; then the winds fill them up and they disappear. As you move east down the beach, the current slackens and the water becomes more shoal.

I remember one good summer day, after lunch at Westward Ho, our elders loaded the cars with six or so of us kids and some aunts and uncles and we headed out for Smith Point. As a six-year-old, that the point was named for my grandparents, Smith, I took for granted. Grandparents were important people, and the point was close to their house. On the way, we went past Milly's ice cream stand. My grandfather liked ice cream, too, so stopping for cones was part of the expedition.

With the crowd of us, there was quite a bit of organization to get us in an ordered line for the treat. Milly expected us to say "Please" and "Thank you" upon asking for and receiving the cone. The rule was, you could not have a cone if you did not say the words. We wanted the ice cream and would have said anything. "Please" and "Thank you" were not difficult. But I made the mistake of thinking you were to say "Please" when you asked and "Thank you" after you received.

So, when my turn came, I said "Please." Milly proffered the cone but then snatched it back from me as I did not say my thanks while it was still under control in her hand. Give her credit, setting, as she was, an example for the parents, because she was paying attention to them, rather than to me, and she moved prematurely. Nonetheless, snatching it away, she broke the cone. The fuss subsided, but I did not forgive her.

Tuckernuck

Tuckernuck consists of an eroding morainal deposit, the north side of which tidal currents have built up with sand accretions. On the north shore of the island there are three ponds, one in the east and two in the west. The ponds, or more properly lagoons—as they are joined to the sea—were created by spits which grew to nearly enclose them. In the southeast corner is a fourth lagoon. It is known as The Lagoon and is the harbor for Tuckernuck. The Lagoon shelters the principal landing for Tuckernuck, and in summer an occasional ferry service runs from Hither Creek.

Extensive sand banks run for about two miles north of the island with depths of one-half to five feet, part of a system that extends from Muskeget Channel to the Eel Point channel. These banks are full of shellfish and effectively block boat traffic to the north shore. A reminder is the wreck of an English trawler which blew aground in a winter gale 30 years ago, reportedly trying to land a cargo of illicit drugs.

Tuckernuck's south shore is subject to strong erosion. The overall battle between erosion and accretion is not in Tuckernuck's favor, as the island today is a third smaller than it was in 1900. The south shore is subject to strong longshore currents which are caused by two tidal waves, about four hours out of phase, interfering here, which creates large differences in water level short distances apart. The sands moved by these currents rapidly create and destroy large spits and islands of sand. Smith Point, Bigelows Point, and the Gravelly Islands have come, gone, and partially come back again. The net result is negative. In the past few years, Bigelows Point has built out more than a mile towards Muskeget. Who knows how long it will remain.

Tuckernuck is inhabited in the summer by about a hundred people. Before Nantucket became a posh resort in the 1980s, the more reclusive islander would retreat to Madaket for the summer months, leaving town to the summer people. Today a few of this sort remove themselves to Tuckernuck to experience their summer without the glitz and bustle that Nantucket imports from New York, London, and Paris during July and August. Tuckernuck's is a tight-knit group of residents who know each other well and have been there for a long time. They enjoy their peace and quiet. Ed Coffin has written a good social history of Tuckernuck for those interested in learning more about it.[1]

---

1. Coffin, *Tuckernuck Island.*

THE LAGOON

APPROACH: Follow the channel out from Eel Point, past the end of Smith Point. After Smith Point, pay careful attention to the current running in and out at several knots through the cut, which might sweep you either out to sea over Bonita Bar or onto the banks to the north.

Just short of the north end of the secondary spit a buoy marking the south end of the entrance bar is sometimes there and sometimes not! This is the fan bar caused by tide running in and out of the cove. This bar is highly elongated by the strong longshore current that runs here. Turn to the north around the end of the bar. Look at the water, not the buoy, because the buoy, if it is even there, is not exactly at the end of the bar. Sailing close along the spit (10 yards), turn west after reaching its end to enter the cove. The depths inside the cove are 10 feet or more.

BOTTOM: Sandy mud. Good holding.

CURRENTS: None. But there is a tidal anomaly here. High and low water occur 3 hours *before* Boston, which is 3 hours and 40 minutes different from Eel Point—only 2.5 miles away—and 4 hours different from Nantucket Harbor.

PROTECTION: The Lagoon is completely protected from all directions. It is quite dramatic, as the open Atlantic is just 100 yards away across Whale Point. On a rough day the surf is loud and close.

DESCRIPTION: The Lagoon is a deep, well-protected cove on the southeast end of Tuckernuck. It is formed by two sand spits, a primary one separating it from the open Atlantic to the south and a secondary one extending northwards from the first, partially closing off its entrance from Madaket Harbor. The cove is not easy to enter but, once inside, is effectively landlocked. It has a wood pier used for landing people and supplies to Tuckernuck. There is good anchorage anywhere in the cove. Keep clear of the wood pier and the moorings in the northwest corner.

The West End. Hither Creek in foreground left, with Esthers and Tuckernuck beyond.
Eel Point is to the right, with Tuckernuck Bank beyond. Muskeget in the distance.
Photo © Garth Grimmer.

Muskeget

Today, Muskeget is a sandbar created and moved about by the tides from the debris of the original island, which was a lump of glacial moraine. Morainal Muskeget was destroyed by a late eighteenth-century hurricane. Muskeget's destruction occurred before Des Barres' chart was drawn, so there is no good record of the island's original position; but it was reported that the storm moved it three miles northeastwards, near its present position.

Muskeget is abandoned today, but in the nineteenth and twentieth centuries it was frequented for hunting and fishing and used as a rescue outpost. Ed Coffin has written a book about Muskeget, detailing its history.[2]

Today there is no harbor or preferred landing place on Muskeget. Historically there has often been a sand spit extended off the southwest corner of Muskeget, which enclosed a shallow lagoon that was used as a harbor. That spit has been gone for a while. Today there is an elongated sand island a quarter-mile south of Muskeget. Perhaps it will join up with the south point and make the harbor again. In good weather the shoal water of the banks makes it possible to land a small boat on the beach or to anchor in still water and go ashore. Muskeget and the dry shoals near it are frequented by the hordes of grey seals that pester Nantucket today.

I sailed to Muskeget some time ago in *Magic*, an Alerion Class Sloop. She draws a scant 29 inches of water, so she allowed me to approach the island from the north following a swale through the banks. It was a light day and I anchored just off the north shore. The harbor on the south side existed then, but it was too shallow for even *Magic*. I had a difficult moment when the wind died and the swell brought *Magic* up to the beach. She hit bottom about three yards from shore on a cobble bottom! The swells bounced

---

2. Coffin, *Muskeget, Nantucket's Forgotten Island*.

her up and down on the cobbles, which was hard on her bottom, but it allowed me to push her off when she was afloat on top of the waves. It could have ended differently. I wondered where the cobbles came from. Are they part of the glacial moraine, or were they dumped there from some earlier shipwreck, since disappeared?

Muskeget and the outer reaches of the Tuckernuck banks are a bit of wilderness quite close by. They are lonely, remote, and unfrequented. Venturers there will be rewarded by the beauty and solitude, but they will be on their own.

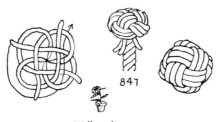

Wall and crown

11

Around the Island

Ketch

The notion of voyaging stretches back into the soft focused reaches of a bookish child's vivid imagination.

—Silver Donald Cameron, *Sniffing the Coast*

To sail around Nantucket is both to take a cruise and to make a passage. Nantucket has two shores: the concave north one facing the Sound with many stopping places and the convex south one facing the ocean which lacks any landing at all. We can cruise the concavity, but the convex side must be sailed along. *At it* we may look, but *on it* we can land only at our peril. Indeed, hundreds of vessels have mislanded on the outer convex shore of the Island; their resting spots are well described in *Wrecks Around Nantucket:*

> Many a noble vessel, never heard from after leaving port, has laid her bones upon the dangerous shoals which intervene between the South Shoal Lightship and Nantucket. Parts of vessels have drifted ashore, from time to time, ... Upon various buildings on the island the name of some ill-fated vessel, the figure head, or a portion thereof, may be seen displayed—striking reminders of the shipwrecks and disasters that have occurred upon our shores.[1]

1. Gardner, *Wrecks Around Nantucket,* from the introduction to the 1877 edition.

OPPOSITE: Yawl *Starry Night* circumnavigates Nantucket. Photo © Garth Grimmer.

Nantucket's outer shoreline of spectacular beaches is inhospitable to boats.

I have made the sail around twice, once in 1976 aboard *Queen Jane*, a modified Cuthbert and Cassion 24-foot Shark. She was a fin keeler drawing 3 feet. She mitigated her lack of engine with very good sailing performance. And a second time aboard *Starry Night*, in the summer of 2013. *Starry Night* is a 40-foot cruising boat drawing 3.5 feet. She is a swift, able yawl, with a cozy cabin built in sympathy with the traditions of the sea. On this voyage she is manned by the Doctor, the Commodore, and myself, three old friends.

Starry Night has left Nantucket harbor at 3:30 on an August afternoon. It is a typical summer day, clear and southwesterly force 4 to 5. Running out the channel, we reef at can "7" and at nun "2" harden up for the beat out to Eel Point. On a day like this, much of the breeze is caused by the land. The farther away you are from Brant Point the less of it there is. By the time we reach the West End, the wind has dropped to a very pleasant force 3.

We are headed for our evening destination, the Lagoon, a near landlocked cove at the southeastern corner of Tuckernuck. There one is as close to the Atlantic as one can be while still sheltered by the land. On my earlier circumnavigation the Lagoon did not exist. On that trip I stopped for the night just northeast of Eel Point in the little pocket protected by the shoals of the Eel Point channel. North Point itself was not nearly so developed then as it is today, but the weather had been mild and our overnight turned out pleasantly.

I planned today's trip so that the tide would be at half water, and flooding, when we would reach the Eel Point red bell "2." I wished to sail through Eel Point channel both against the current and with a rising tide. *Starry Night* draws only 3.5 feet, but it is shallow at the West End and it is easy to make a mistake. If we were to run aground, I wanted the current, which is strong here, to be pushing us off, not onto, whatever we had run into. And I wished

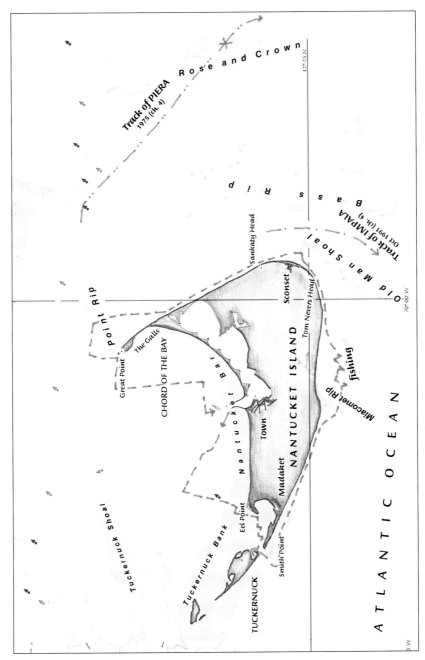

Track of *Starry Night* around Nantucket Island

to be able to look forward to a rising tide to lift us off. I have been here several times in *Impala*, a large boat for Madaket, drawing 8 feet. The passage should be much easier with *Starry Night* than it had been with her. But I am not eager to make a fool of myself by running the Commodore or the Doctor aground. They are both experienced mariners who know the waters well.

We tack around the bell and head in towards the Eel Point beach on starboard tack, close hauled to keep off the shoal to leeward. The sun, reflecting off the wavelets, sprinkles sparkles across the water to the southwest hiding the next buoys in a glare of scintillation. The Eel Point channel buoys are small plastic town marks, less visible than their federal cousins; they are hard to see even in the best light. In the 1950s and 1960s, before the Eel Point bell was established, there was a triangular wood pyramid near the end of Eel Point which was a beacon for this leg. If you approached the beacon from the correct bearing, it would bring you through the outer reach of the channel. But ever since 1961, when hurricane Esther broke through and fashioned Esthers Island from Smith Point, the Eel Point channel, North Point, and the shoals associated with it have become much more extensive and complex. The beacon is gone now; the buoys serve in its place.

We sail "blind" for three-quarters of a mile, trusting our compass, till we come close enough to see the first red buoy and shortly thereafter espy the dry shoal (a tiny island at low tide) behind it that forces a dogleg in our route. We sail past that little nun till we are almost on the sand. There, we flip over onto port tack, just able to fetch (and see) the next marks a half-mile ahead to the west. A green can marks the west end of the second dry shoal, and a red nun, just beyond it to leeward, is to keep you from overshooting the turn and running onto the extensive Tuckernuck flats lying to the west. We go a little by the can and tack over onto starboard, heading now for the end of Eel Point.

The shoals on the east side of the channel are quite abrupt. Deep water of 8 to 10 feet runs right up close to them. After the second turn of the channel, they run continuously all the way to the point. Although the channel is wide here near the point, a finger of shoal starts in its middle. The finger creates a deceptively deep west branch, which, in fact, dead ends in a bar. Consequently it is important to stay on the east side of the channel near the visible shallow water of the dry shoals.

We sail *Starry Night* close into and along the Eel Point beach. The bustle of Nantucket is behind us. The north shore of Eel Point is a beautiful area of recently formed and rapidly changing land, generated by the Esthers Island breakthrough. Large arms of sand have formed and enclosed patches of water, making a highly intertwined complex of sea, sand, creek, and pond. The building of North Point has demonstrated the process, in high speed, that long ago built East and North Ponds on Tuckernuck, Haulover Pond, Great Point and its pond, and other parts of Nantucket. On this sparkling summer afternoon the sand is bright. The air has the "salt" smell. This smell is actually that of dimethyl sulfide exuding from plankton being devoured by the denizens of the shore. The sea is clean, filling with the new water of a flooding tide.

We move past Eel Point quickly. Protected by the shoal water all around us, we are in smooth water. Right past Eel Point the channel bifurcates at an abrupt "T." A west branch runs to Tuckernuck and an east branch leads into Madaket's Hither Creek. The shoal that forces the turn is right before us as we come in past the point. It is a foot deep and must be respected. It is sometimes marked by a small ball float. The Commodore sees the mark, and we tack to the west at the appropriate moment.

We are now beyond the formal town buoyage and must find our way between the flats of Esthers Island (today, connected and properly called Smith Point) to our south and the extreme shoal waters of Tuckernuck flats to our north. There are two informal marks—round fishing floats—that locals have set to guide the Tuckernuck ferry, but we cannot see them yet. We short tack along a median course of 270 degrees for a mile till we find the first. Leaving it to starboard we know we are on route and that it is pretty much clear water all the rest of way to the Lagoon.

The Lagoon is formed by Whale Point, an inlet spit projecting from Tuckernuck. Smith Point is its complement, projecting out from Madaket. Between them the tidal streams run in and out to sea, forming a classic tidal inlet. This one, oddly, considering its importance, has no name. The cut separates Nantucket from Tuckernuck. The next easily navigable opening, Muskeget Channel, is nine miles farther west near Martha's Vineyard. As is usual the mouth of the opening is partially blocked, here by Bonita Bar, a very good fishing spot exploited both by small boats and by surf-casters working off the beach at the tip of Smith Point. Bonita Bar almost touches Smith Point, separated by a tiny channel that hugs the south shore beach as it runs easterly out to the sea.

As we sail by this evening, the Bar is its usual spectacle. A light swell is moving in from the southwest to meet the current and shallow water at Smith Point. Even though the current is flowing with the swell, the swells pyramid into a topsy-turvy, gurgling, hissing jumble.

The Doctor has fished this Bar and he knows that the fish, for which it was named, are here. The Commodore has been around long enough to know that with an outgoing current and a stronger wind the Bar is a dangerous place. The waves might be four or five times the height, and just as irregular, as they are on this idyllic evening. The combination of wild seas and good fishing has brought mishap and near tragedy to these waters recurrently. Yet their danger does nothing to detract from their beauty.

We plan to spend tonight in the Lagoon and sail through the cut in the morning. The Lagoon, formed by the inlet spit, Whale Point, extending eastwards from Tuckernuck, is further formed by a secondary spit extending north from the tip of Whale Point, partially closing off the mouth of the bay formed by the primary spit. There is strong longshore transport running north here trying to close off the remaining opening, but the current outflowing the cove prevents it from doing so. There is the usual fan of dumped material partially blocking the opening.

The entrance channel is narrow and crooked but 6 feet deep, plenty for *Starry Night*—if we can manage to stay within its bounds. To enter the cove we must wriggle around behind the fan, so we head directly for the beach, 75 yards south of the spit's north end. Fifteen yards short of the beach we take a hard right around a ball marking (well, sort of marking—we alter our route a little judging the color of the water) the end of the fan. Then we sail north till just past the end of the spit and take a hard left turning west into the cove. Inside, the water is 10 to 12 feet deep. Before Whale Spit formed, this area was the channel, scoured deep by the current. Now surrounded by arms of sand, the pool retains much of its original depth. Tonight it is as still as a pond, which it almost is.

Starry Night is a big boat for the Lagoon, so we feel our way into the cove towards the south beach, moving slowly past the dock where a couple of open boats are moored. I'd never had a depth sounder in here before. I am surprised that we are able to put the bow on the beach, yet the stern is in 10 feet of water. We anchor, in fact, too close to shore. The dying breeze might well come up northerly during the night and set us ashore. So up comes the anchor. We drift back 50 yards and drop it again.

It is a beautiful end to a beautiful afternoon. In the quiet of the evening, the Commodore and I dive over and swim to the beach. We walk across the spit and dive again into the surf on the ocean side. Both waters are 78 degrees, the tropical warmth that Nantucket may enjoy for a few days in a good August. We swim back to the boat and as we dry off, the sun sets. Overhead, bankers on weekend release are making approach in their jets to Nantucket's airport, an intermediate stop on their way to long-prearranged cocktail gatherings.

Through the entrance to the cove another sort of escapee approaches. A sailor works his catboat in and around the spit to his preferred anchorage 200 yards east of us. We recognize him as an old acquaintance. He sets up his boat for the night and settles into dinner with his wife. Their conversation, beyond our hearing, is accompanied by the soothing sounds of a ceaseless sea seething against the sands of a resort of utter tranquility, decorated by stars emerging from a dying twilight. Other than stars, the only lights are *Starry Night*'s anchor light and the twinkle of Nantucket, far away.

I won't go into what we ate for dinner, nor what we drank, nor the tales we told. Suffice to say, after a pleasant evening and a good night's sleep, we awake in the morning, after sunup, break our fast, and get under way. The morning is grey, cooler than yesterday. The wind is light, force 3 westerly—a good breeze for our purpose of making passage down the back side of Nantucket.

Now it is, generally, easier to leave an anchorage than to enter it. In the first place, you know where you are starting from, and, secondly, all you have to do is retrace your successful path in from the evening before. Unfortunately, with ease comes complacency. We put *Starry Night* aground just outside the end of the entrance spit. We have misjudged and cut the corner a little too close. Fortunately a full cycle of the tide has elapsed and the current is pulling us off. We are soon away, beyond the barrier bar and headed out through the cut towards the open sea.

The channel out to sea runs close to Whale Point on the west side of the opening. It is deep, scoured by the strong current. Two hundred yards past Whale Point the current eases and the usual fan of deposited sand occurs. There is a line of breakers on the fan which appears to be a continuous barrier across the opening. Within the channel the water is rough, with such a bopple of waves that *Starry Night* can make little headway against the current, hard on the light wind as we are, so I use an assist from her engine.

I have not been through here in a keel boat since the *Queen Jane* trip 38 years before, but the Doctor has done it many times fishing. He guides us to the westwards, inside the line of breakers, till a quarter-mile west of Whale Point we outflank them and proceed south to deep water. The least water depth, I estimate from our depth sounder, has been 8 feet, at half tide, so it is a pretty deep channel.

A note on the tide here: between Eel Point and the Lagoon, a distance of 2.5 miles, the time of high water differs by 3.7 hours. This is caused by the tidal wave inflooding from the sea and interacting with the other two tidal waves dominant in the Sound. Needless to say, it causes strong and anomalous currents. There is a two-foot difference in water level between Eel Point and the Lagoon two hours after high water in Boston. And as we were trying to push out the western arm of the cut that morning, the water was two and a half feet higher a mile and a half up the beach on the Tuckernuck south shore. No wonder it took *Starry Night*'s entire nine horsepower to make headway. We were going uphill!

Having made it through the cut without being swept by breakers, we bear off onto a broad reach for an easy passage along Madaket's south shore. The outer shore of Nantucket shore runs from here in a smooth convex curve for 23 miles to Great Point. Its beach is one of the great places to swim or surf on the east coast of North America. But it has no place for a sailing boat to stop. Being convex, there is no shelter. We will keep moving. We sail in towards Long Pond beach keeping about 200 yards offshore. It is easy sailing, and with the beach gradually curving away from us I must pay attention, at the helm, to neither wander too far offshore nor, far worse, to sidle into the surf zone. We wish to sail close, but not too close because the edge of the surf zone is not fixed. On a shelving beach like this one a larger set of waves may quietly surprise the unwary by breaking to seaward of them and washing them into disaster.

It has become a grey day and at 10:00 a.m. the beachers are yet to arrive. We have this beautiful waterscape entirely to ourselves. Nantucket Island comes to an abrupt end here at the south shore. There is a bluff that drops down 5 to 10 feet to the beach, which itself slopes another 10 feet down to the sea. From the water's edge, a surf zone about 5 feet deep runs out about 100 yards; then the bottom quickly drops off to 70 feet or so, the beginning of the continental shelf. The Doctor, the Commodore, and I have many happy memories of this beach—friends, swimming, romantic evenings. But from a sailboat offshore, it is a lonely place, even a little hostile.

About 11:30 we approach Miacomet Rip. The rip at Miacomet is a bar projecting from the beach a mile and a half into the sea that breaks the smooth line of the shore. The bar is formed by two waves of tide that refract around Nantucket Shoals and come together to deposit their sands. The rip is not only a lonely place, it is a dangerous one. The bar, created by the refraction of the long wave of the tide, itself refracts the shorter ocean swells. Even on a calm day random "rogue" waves will suddenly emerge from a gentle sea to wet the mariner or even capsize his boat. The erratic waves also stir up bait fish, so Miacomet Rip is a good place to fish. Almost all the traffic here is composed of fishing boats which have come from the other, protective, side of the Island.

The Doctor does not let our location go to waste. Out comes his fishing rod and he promptly hooks a five-pound blue. We are sailing along fast, so I bring *Starry Night* up into the wind and heave her to on the other tack. All to no avail because, in our maneuvers, the fish gets away. The Doctor is patient. He casts around the mizzen rigging, which is definitely in his way. In the next hour, as we approach Tom Nevers Head, the Doctor hooks four more fish. There are plenty of them out here! But we land none, either because we do not stop quickly enough or because, lacking a landing net, we cannot get the fish aboard over the lifelines. The Doctor says, "Enough of this. Let's get on our way." The sky is getting darker. It looks like rain.

So off we go heading in towards the shore at Tom Nevers Head. I am surprised to see the mansions crowding the Head. When I was a child and we played on this bluff, it was deserted. When I circumnavigated the Island in 1975, the entire south shore of Nantucket had but three or four houses visible from the sea and none at Tom Nevers. This trip, houses have been continuous, one every hundred feet or so. In Madaket they are even falling over the edge as the sea erodes the land from underneath them. From Smith Point to Miacomet the erosion is severe. During the past 40 years, the south shoreline has receded as much as 1,000 feet. At the rate it is going, I am going to have to look for a new island in 400 years! At any rate, Tom Nevers Head is today wall-to-wall houses, two and a half stories high. The development stops at Tom Nevers Pond and leaves a gap along Low Beach before houses appear again in Sconset.

Out to sea from us, Old Man Shoal is breaking. From the direction we are coming, Old Man is the first of the famous Nantucket Shoals that extend out 40 miles to Asia Rip. The shoals run in more or less concentric bands parallel to the shore. We sail in close to shore, just inside Old Man, and have broken water on both sides of us till we are abeam of Sconset. The narrow unmarked channel between the Low Beach Bar and Old Man is much easier to find coming from the west. It is difficult to discern coming from the north, as you will remember from *Impala*'s 1990 experience related in chapter 5, when we had to take her outside Old Man and suffer another 5 miles of shoal water uncertainty before reaching open water.

The shoreline bends rapidly here. At Sconset we change our course from east-northeast to northwest. The shore is steep and the current is strong. The tide refracts around the lens of Nantucket Shoals with a wave coming in from both the north and the south. The interfering waves have a node at Tom Nevers and a peak at Great Point. The time of high water is about the same all along this shore, but the range varies considerably. At both high and low tide there is a one-foot difference in water level between Tom Nevers and Quidnet. This sets up a strong longshore current, which runs hardest at the normal time of slack water. This is the current that moves a lot of sand to Miacomet Rip and to Point Rip up at Great Point.

While we aboard *Starry Night* are thinking about all this oceanography, it starts to rain. Now you would think that with a combined maritime experience in Nantucket waters of almost 200 years, the crew would have brought more than one set of foul weather gear, even in August. I am sorry to say that, in this case, you would have been wrong. So we start up the eastern shore of Nantucket with myself at the helm in the only set aboard, the Commodore toughing it out on deck, and the Doctor under cover in the companion. It takes about five minutes of rain to get the Commodore wet enough for discretion to overwhelm valor; he, too, goes below.

About 10 minutes later both come out on deck as we pass by, close in to the beach, the eroding cliffs of Sankaty. Although the engineering works being used to try to stabilize the bluff are difficult to ascertain, the erosion is clear enough. I am surprised at how localized it is. I expected the whole thing, from just north of Codfish Park to well past the lighthouse, to be a raw edge of tumbling dirt. In reality, this is so only for about 600 yards. North of Sankaty Light the sand dunes are also drifting back, although in less spectacular fashion.

Life ashore in Sconset, begun in the 1890s by theater people from New York City, is dainty and dignified. The mansions above overlook the beach but do not use it. Their view is of the horizon beyond the sea. Other than the tumbling cliff behind it, the shore here is unremarkable. The beach is narrow and, at high tide, almost entirely wet by wave swash. The water is deep even close into the beach, and strong currents sweep up and down the shore, making for poor swimming. Although the beach has a raw beauty here, beachcombers are rare.

Our day has turned dreary, even cold. It is early August, but this is New England. The wind is still from the west, off the land, force 3 and 4. The rain is steady, the sea calm. *Starry Night* has come to a place where few sailboats venture. We take the opportunity to cruise close into the shore past Quidnet, Squam, Wauwinet, and outer Coskata beaches, which are the most remote and beautiful on the Island. On a prettier day, I would sail this way 50 yards off the beach all the way to Great Point. Then if I felt brave I might even round the point close in, through the tiny channel across the rip 100 yards out from the point. We actually did all that in *Queen Jane* 38 years ago. We even anchored for lunch just outside the close break at Coskata. But even though the conditions were near perfect then, there was a subtle swell that kept *Queen Jane* rolling. It was beautiful, but not very comfortable.

But today, with the cold and rain and a crew holed up below, we are not in the mood for such an explore. I leave the beachside at Wauwinet and head out into the gloom for can "1" near the end of Point Rip. More visible than the can, which is beyond all shallow water and hard to see from a distance, are the breakers that jump up at certain points on the rip. The rip looks on the chart like a long ridge curving out from Great Point. In fact, it is a series of knolls projecting above a deeper bar. The tops of the knolls come almost to the water's surface. The low swell refracts, reverses its direction, and crashes into itself causing breakers to swirl in all directions around the high spots. Yet most of the rip remains quiet and seven or eight feet deep. We find and sail around the outermost of the broken patches. A hundred yards later we are in the deep water of Great Round Shoal Channel, and can "1" is clearly visible behind us to starboard, just where it ought to be.

Crossing the rip, we go back hard on the wind, which is blowing straight from Nantucket Harbor eight miles away. I short tack in to look at Great Point as best I can. Great Point is a favorite place for surfcasting fishermen. It has all the attributes of a good fishing spot: remote, hard to get to, beautiful, and full of fish. For the same reasons, Great Point is very attractive to seals, who through the perversity of our laws are driving the fishermen out. We sail by on starboard tack close enough in to see that there are no picnics today. Then the land forces us to tack away.

The best way to see Great Point by sail is to be going the other direction. Leave Nantucket in a westerly by sailing out through the cut in the East Jetty and cruise 20 yards from the water's edge along the seven curving miles of Coatue Beach all the way to the end. Then when you go past the tip of the point you can do as we are doing, harden up for the beat back to home. On the beat home you may well come to the U.S. Coast Guard's mooring buoy in Chord of the Bay (approx. position 41°21.7'N, 70°05.0'W). This is a large white nun that probably weighs 5,000 pounds. It is neither lit nor marked on the chart. Undoubtedly the Coast Guard knows where it is, and I imagine it shows up on radar. It is definitely a hazard.

About 4:00 p.m., as a token of His beneficence, the sky starts to clear. We are approaching Nantucket Bar bell, the outer marker for Nantucket Harbor. The Commodore and the Doctor, who have been sailing since Point Rip, are starting to warm up, and our voyage is coming to its happy end. We have had a good trip with a variety of conditions. The voyage took in its entirety 24 hours. During that time, we have sailed 40 miles and spent one night in the wilderness. Of those 24 hours we have sailed for 10 and been under power for a quarter.

As the reader can see from our story, the route is one not without peril. Bonita Bar is a dangerous place; the back side of Nantucket is remote from rescue and devoid of traffic. But our voyage is one that a competent sailor can make, and if he does, he will long remember it with satisfaction.

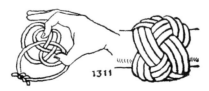

Turk's head

12

Boats

Whitehall rowboat

A yacht owner is an individualist who shares only one obsession with his fellow yachtsman. The boat he owns is the best he or anybody else ever had.

—Alfred F. Loomis, preface to *The Hotspur Story*

THERE ARE TWO rules that apply to cruising boats:

First Rule of Boats: The smaller your boat the more fun you have.

Second Rule of Boats: You can have fun in a larger boat if it does not draw too much water.

To explore, we want for a boat. To explore closely and well, we want for a shallow and nimble boat. We will wish to carry gear, friends, and maybe even overnight shelter, so we want for a boat of some capacity. This is clearly in conflict with rule one; unfortunately boats must be compromises—just don't compromise on draft.

A good cruising boat needs three qualities. She should be reliable to get the sailor there and back without a stop for breakdowns. She should be easy to sail because the purpose of a cruise is to explore the edge undistracted by complications of gear and rig. And she should be a good sailer because a fine sailing boat peacefully lulls the sailor into the proper frame of mind for contemplation of the natural marvels his cruise will set before him.

The catboat, the traditional workboat of Nantucket, met all these needs. According to Chapelle, catboats began (early nineteenth century) as normally proportioned fishing boats similar to Noank sloops of Connecticut.[1] Then, as their fisherman owners started racing them, their beam increased to half their length, the draft decreased, and their single gaff rigged main sail plans enlarged. This made the cats fast, but cranky to sail. They could carry a heavy weather helm, which is due not to the usual mis-located rig but rather to the unbalanced hull shape—sharp forward with extreme beam aft. They were given large "barn door" rudders, which, along with strong helmsmen, kept them going straight.

The catboats' position in Nantucket is well described by Clint Andrews:

> At the end of the Gay Nineties, Nantucket was well known, up and down the coast as the home of the big catboats. A fleet of approx-imately forty boats, each between twenty-five and thirty-five feet long, was owned and sailed here. Only two or three were private boats. Most carried sailing, picnic, and fishing parties in summer and fished for scallops in winter. A small number were used for cod and mackerel fishing in season.[2]

In the twentieth century many were rigged with engines. In the 1960s they were abandoned and replaced by outboard runabouts: a cheaper, faster, albeit less seaworthy alternative.

Catboats, even after their racing development, still make fairly good cruisers. Their great beam makes for large carrying capac-ity and stability, both desirable features for cruising. Their shoal draft, of course, is their most important dimension for exploring the interaction of land and sea. Because of the beam and lack of

---

1. Chapelle, *American Small Sailing Craft*, 252–256.
2. Andrews, *Fishing around Nantucket*, 11.

Catboats at the Steamboat Wharf, their crews drying sails and gamming. Courtesy of the Nantucket Historical Association.

overhangs, a catboat over 20 feet long is a large boat. In 1912 Henry Plumber made a seven-month voyage from New Bedford to Florida in his 24-foot catboat, *Mascot*, spinning the yarn for posterity in *Me, the Boy, and the Cat*.[3] Although he had many adventures along the way, none was caused by the boat being too small.

True to their racing heritage, catboats are fast. In 2009 the 28-foot *Kathleen*, a replica of a 1917 racing cat, won the Opera House Cup, 92 years after her design was laid down. They also teach the basics. Since 1921 five generations of southern New England sailors have learned sailing and racing in the 12-foot Beetle Cat, designed and built by New Bedford's Beetle family, who got started building whaleboats in the nineteenth century. A large fleet of Beetle Cats exists in Nantucket, where they are known as "Rainbows" because of their multicolored sails. The Rainbows are fun boats to race, but they also are fun boats just to sail. I first got my hands on one at age 11, and that summer I began a life of cruising by making voyages and spending nights in the confines of Nantucket Harbor on these wonderful little boats. Each year, before the Opera House Cup, the Rainbows demonstrate their nickname by parading their multicolored sails around Brant Point.

The Marshall 18 is another catboat class that came to Nantucket in the 1960s. Built by Marshall Marine in Padanarem, it is a small version of the classic Cape Cod catboat which is used for racing in Nantucket Harbor and cruising Island waters. It has the standard catboat advantages for doing so.

Not all the racing classes are suited for cruising. Racing pleasure derives from besting your competitors, which is quite different from the pleasure of cruising, which derives from learning from the interaction of the land and sea. Racing generates a different sort of boat. Although irrational in a one-design fleet, comfort, seaworthiness, and practicality are highly compromised in racing

---

3. Plumber, *Me, the Boy, and the Cat*.

classes in favor of speed. While most cruising boats are fun to race, few race boats are good for cruising.

A good case in point is Nantucket's Flying Dutchman Class, which was established with the delivery of 32 boats in 1958. The FD is a high-performance light displacement dinghy sailed by a crew of two, one of whom hangs beyond the edge of the boat on a trapeze. I have sailed mine at over 15 knots, and they are reputed to go as fast as 20. Exhilarating to sail, they are too unstable and too fast (see powerboats, below) to be any good for cruising. The crew's attention is entirely directed to keeping them upright; no time remains for contemplation or discovery. Soon after the fleet was introduced here, it became an Olympic Class. The 1959 Pan Am eliminations and U.S. Nationals were hosted in Head of the Harbor. By 1970 the boats were mostly gone, too specialized for all but semi-pros and useful only for competition.

Nantucket has had a series of larger deep drafted keel boats that have been used for racing outside the harbor. In the 1920s and 1930s there were the Vineyard Sound Interclubs. In the 1950s and 1960s they were replaced by the Yankee One Design. Today the International One Design is used. Excluded from the delightful waters of Up Harbor and the West End by their deep draft, these classes have generated wet and uncomfortable racing thrills on Nantucket for almost a century. And for the six days of the week that are not race days, they grace the mooring field with their sleek beauty.

The Alerion Class Sloop is a counter example. The Alerion Class Sloop was introduced to Nantucket in 1977 by my brother, Edward, and me. We have built 29 of them at five locations on the Island, the Cape, and San Francisco. Although most were sold "abroad" to the continental United States, many of those have returned to the Island under later ownership. The Alerion Class Sloop has become a racing class, but her original purpose was to be an exquisite pleasure sailing boat. She was designed by the famous Nat Herreshoff. He built her for his personal use in his later years. She has the draft of a catboat but not the extreme beam, so her sailing grace is uncompromised. She is stable, fast, and dry. She makes a good racing boat but is far better suited to cruising, perfect for exploring the ins and outs of Nantucket's waters. My elegant cousin Jodie once said, "When I sail aboard her, I feel like Princess Grace."

The purpose of this quick survey of boats that have been popular in Nantucket is to show that the controlling dimension is draft. A boat drawing more than 4 feet is for practical purposes excluded from sailing up harbor or at the West End. You can, as we learned in chapter 9, carry 5 feet all the way to Wauwinet. But you can do so only by meticulously holding to the channel and bypassing the interesting landing spots. The delights of Up Harbor become a tease rather than a reward. I personally have taken my *Impala*, which draws a majestic 8 feet, through the Eel Point channel to the mouth of Tuckernuck's Lagoon. Perhaps with luck I could have continued and passed out to sea past the Bonita Bar. But a small misstep making such an exit could well result in the loss of the boat. Nor could *Impala* enter the Lagoon to enjoy its tranquility. No, 3.5 feet is the practical draft limit for cruising around Nantucket, and 2 feet is liberating.

Can you cruise by powerboat? Well, it can be done, although it rarely is. At first glance a powerboat has the features required, shoal draft and easy maneuvering. A good powerboat is dependable and can be counted on to get you home in a calm. The big drawback of powerboats is that they go too fast.

When a boat starts to move faster (in knots) than 1.1 times the square root of her waterline (in feet) it begins to rise up on its bow wave and use a lot of power. For a 25-footer this speed is about 5.5 knots. Very few motorboats are run so slowly. At speed, the vibration, noise, and bounce mean the only person who is having fun is the one behind the throttle. Those hanging on at higher speeds are traveling too fast through the waterscape to explore it. The waterscape itself is disrupted by the wake.

I remember arriving at Amelia Island, Florida, during a sailing cruise through the Intracoastal Waterway. I was aboard motor-less *Queen Jane.* Touching up her paint at the dock, I got into a conversation with a waterborne state policeman. His "cruiser" was a speedboat and he allowed as how it would go 60 miles per hour. I bragged that *Queen Jane* sometimes reached 6 knots. He shook his head. "I don't know about sailboats," he said. "When I go somewhere, I want to *git* there!"

I think he had it about right. When you want to *"git there,"* go by powerboat (preferably as the driver). When you want to be somewhere, when you want to experience the shore, when you want to explore the interaction of the land and sea, try sailing.

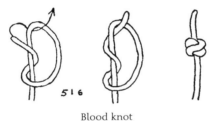

Blood knot

Peaceful end to a peaceful day in a quiet protected cove. *Starry Night* moored in Nantucket, sporting her new 2014 rig. Photo © Garth Grimmer.

APPENDIX
Beaufort Scale

YOU MAY HAVE noticed that several times in this book I use the force numbers of the Beaufort Scale to describe wind speeds. The Beaufort Scale was popularized by Admiral Francis Beaufort of the Royal Irish Navy in 1805. People ask in this age of digital instruments, why use it? Why not just give the wind speed in knots? The reason is intrinsic in the very nature of the wind itself.

The wind is the general movement of air molecules. Each of these molecules differs in motion, both speed and direction, which has caused at least one prominent physicist to ask, "Does the wind have a velocity?" Good question. For sailors, and for practical purposes, what we mean by wind speed involves two averages: firstly, the average of all the different molecules' motions in some small region around our boat and secondly, the average of these molecules over time. What we mean by wind force is the force the wind exerts on our boat. That force derives from the temperature as well. At the same speed, cold air exerts more force than warm.

Our wonderfully precise digital meters (reading out to the tenth of a knot!) take a small sample (near the rotor cups) of all the air around us and average it over a short time (a few seconds). So when the log keeper writes "wind speed 11.8 knots," he is saying that there was a packet of air near the mast head moving for a few seconds at that speed. True, perhaps, but probably irrelevant.

One of the first things a sailor learns is that the wind is not constant, even on a steady day. It has lulls and puffs. The intelligent log keeper, rather than writing 11.8 knots, might write in the log "9–12 knots." Notice that the precision of the tenth of a knot has disappeared and a range has taken its place. This is required of any sensible discussion of wind speed. What Beaufort did was standardize the ranges. He did so by taking ranges that were big enough to matter to the sailing of a boat yet small enough to get the nuances of differing conditions.

Furthermore, as speed instruments were not available at the time, Beaufort defined his ranges by *the effect* the force of the wind had on sailing vessels and upon the surface of the sea. Whereas the actual speed of the wind is somewhat ethereal and, indeed, only one of the physical variables that determine the wind's force on his boat, which is what the sailor is concerned with, Beaufort's effects could be directly perceived. Only in modern times, when good measuring instruments became available, have Beaufort's "effects" been translated into wind speeds.

Beaufort's ranges were well chosen, and his descriptions are apt. Over time they have been accepted. The scale is a useful tool by which sailors may communicate. Start using it, and I think you will find you like it.

Beaufort Wind Scale

Force	Force title	Wind speed	Effect on sea surface	Wave height	Effect on an Alerion Class Sloop	Effect on flags
0	Calm	<1	Sea like a mirror.	0	No steerage way.	
1	Light air	1–2	Ruffles with the appearance of scales are formed, but without foam crests.	0	Just sufficient for steerage way.	
2	Light breeze	3–5	Small wavelets, still short but more pronounced. Crests have a glassy appearance and do not break.	½	Boat starts to sail well, small angles of heel.	LIGHT BREEZE · FORCE 2
3	Gentle breeze	6–10	Large wavelets. Crests begin to break. Foam of glassy appearance. Perhaps scattered white horses.	2	Speed reached on reach, heeled to windward.	GENTLE BREEZE · FORCE 3
4	Moderate breeze	11–15	Small waves become longer. Fairly frequent white horses.	4	Full sail breeze spray stars.	MODERATE BREEZE · FORCE 4
5	Fresh breeze	16–20	Moderate waves take a more pronounced form. Many white horses are formed. Chance of some spray.	6	Take first reef.	FRESH BREEZE · FORCE 5
6	Strong breeze	21–26	Larger waves form. White foam crests more extensive everywhere. Probably some spray.	9	Take second reef in mainsail. Ride is boisterous.	STRONG BREEZE · FORCE 6
7	Moderate gale	27–33	Sea heaps up and white foam from breaking waves begins to be blown in streaks along the direction of the wind.	13	Reef or drop jib. Boat becoming overpowered.	SMALL CRAFT
8	Fresh gale	34–40	Moderate high waves of greater length. Edges of crests begin to break into spindrift. The foam blown into well marked streaks along the direction of the wind.	18	Jib down. Take shelter or heave to.	
9	Strong gale	41–47	High waves. Dense streaks of foam along the direction of the wind. Crests of waves begin to topple, tumble, and roll over. Spray may affect visibility.	23	Extra lines on anchors and moorings.	GALE
10	Whole gale	48–55	Very high waves with long overhanging crests. The resulting foam in great patches is blown in dense white streaks along the direction of the wind. On the whole, the surface of the sea takes on a white appearance. The tumbling of the sea becomes heavy and shock-like. Visibility affected.	30	Extra lines on anchors and moorings.	
11	Storm	56–64	Exceptionally high waves (small and medium ships might be lost for a time behind the waves). The sea is completely covered with long white patches of foam lying along the direction of the wind. Everywhere, the edges of waves are blown into froth. Visibility affected.	40 or more	Haul out of water.	STORM
12	Hurricane	>65	Air filled with foam and spray. Sea completely white with driving spray. Visibility very seriously affected.	40 or more	Haul out of water.	HURRICANE

Flag artwork copyright © by Eric Holch, www.ericholch.com

BIBLIOGRAPHY

Andrews, J. Clinton. *Fishing around Nantucket.* Nantucket, MA: Maria Mitchell Association, 1990. Clint Andrews, descended from Proprietors of Nantucket, was one of the last old-time watermen of Nantucket. His book tells what fish there are to catch, where they are, and the techniques used to catch them. The last chapter concerns *Wonoma,* the last surviving Nantucket catboat, built in 1902 and destroyed at the Town's insistence when she was about a hundred years old.

Ashley, Clifford W. *The Ashley Book of Knots.* New York: Doubleday and Co., Inc., 1944. No one else has come close to the scope and detail of this compendium of knots by Clifford Ashley. It contains discussion of the origin, use, and utility of about 3,000 knots, along with instructions for tying them. Ashley is a graphic artist and the book is illustrated with 3,854 hand-drawn diagrams and many pen and ink sketches. Amusingly, Ashley sings the praises of the multi-strand knot named the Star (#727). It is indeed beautiful and difficult to tie, not in the least because Ashley's directions are incorrect! That, in 60 years of using the book, is the only mistake I have found in this colossal work.

Bascom, Willard. *Waves and Beaches.* Watertown, MA: Educational Services Inc., 1964. Subtitled "The dynamics of the ocean surface," this is a succinct discussion of the movement of the ocean's surface and its effects upon the shore. It is written for the layman. And it is very refreshing, today, to read a science book that, rather than preaching a political message, gives one a clear presentation of the elegant beauty of nature and her mechanisms. *See also* Defant, below.

Belloc, Hilaire. *The Cruise of the* Nona. London: Constable & Co Ltd., 1925. Belloc (1870–1953) was a political philosopher and historian. He made fine cruises through the difficult waters of the northern British Isles in small boats and writes well about them.

Cameron, Silver Donald. *Sniffing the Coast.* Toronto: Macmillan, 1993. Cameron is an experienced man with a good eye who has been sailing small boats for a long time in Nova Scotia waters.

Chamberlain, Barbara B. *These Fragile Outposts.* Garden City, NJ: Natural History Press, 1964. I am unaware of any other book that presents the geology of the Cape and Islands so clearly. She focuses mostly on the glacial and post-glacial period. It is an in-depth study for the lay reader.

Chapelle, Howard I. *American Small Sailing Craft.* New York: W. W. Norton, Inc., 1951. In the 1930's Howard Chapelle saw the end coming for sailing ships, their building and design. He spent the next 30 years finding and documenting old sailing vessels while running down their history. He published a series of books documenting sail naval ships, merchant ships, fishing schooners, and privateers. In *American Small Sailing Craft* he documents the small craft that formed the foundation of American maritime culture. Chapelle also wrote *Yacht Designing and Planning,* an excellent primer to small craft design.

Coffin, Edward Wayman. *Tuckernuck Island.* Rockland, ME: Lakeside Printing, 2008.

———. *Muskeget, Nantucket's Forgotten Island.* Owls Head, ME: Tug and Grunt Boatyard, 2001.

    These two books are well-illustrated social histories of Tuckernuck and Muskeget. They are a major portion of the literature on Nantucket's two small companion islands. Coffin is a Nantucket Coffin who has been on and off those islands all his life.

Crèvecoeur, J. Hector St. John de. *Letters from an American Farmer.* London: Thomas Davies, 1783; Mineola, NY: Dover, 2005. This is a well-known traveler's report with a disproportionate amount about Nantucket.

Defant, Albert. *Ebb and Flow.* Ann Arbor: University of Michigan Press, 1958. A more technical study of tides that supplements Bascom (above).

Duxbury, Ken. *Lugworm Island Hopping.* London: Pelham Books, 1976. Duxbury is a water spirit. His *Lugworm* books are a delight to read, his voyages grand, and his wife's patience almost unlimited. He understands shoal draft.

Gardner, Arthur H. *Wrecks Around Nantucket.* New Bedford, MA: Reynolds Printing, 1915, 1943. An extremely thorough compendium of wrecks around the Island, both within the Sound and on the outer shoals. Several editions, each subsequent one updated with the latest disasters. A listing with some description of important wrecks.

Johnson, Irving. *The* Peking *Battles Cape Horn.* New York City, NY, National Maritime Historical Society, 1977. More than any man since Slocum, Johnson joined the new world of amateur ocean cruising with the old world of commercial sail. The *Peking* voyage was his apprenticeship. His influence cannot be overstated. Between her voyages around the world, in the 1950s, Johnson frequently anchored *Yankee* just off Nantucket's ruined wharves. She was a magnificent sight.

Lancaster, Clay. *The Architecture of Historic Nantucket.* New York: McGraw-Hill, 1972. Best survey, in my opinion, of Nantucket's unique architecture. It includes a good history of the development of the historic town.

Lecky, S. T. S., Master Mariner. *"Wrinkles" in Practical Navigation.* New York: John Wiley & Sons, 1890, revised and enlarged edition. A wonderful collection of navigational articles presented in a form common in the nineteenth century, but not so much anymore.

Loomis, Alfred F. *The Hotspur Story.* New York: Dodd Mead & Company, 1954. Loomis (1898–1968) was a sailor and a prominent yachting journalist. He sailed *Hotspur,* built in 1929, up and down the East Coast and as far afield as Greece. *Hotspur* is, today, alive and well, berthed at the Cutts and Case yard in Oxford, Maryland.

Maury, Lt. M. F. *The Physical Geography of the Sea,* 6th ed., London: Thomas Nelson and Sons, 1883. The early oceanographic masterpiece by the man who developed the pilot chart.

Mitchell, Carlton. *Yachtsman's Camera.* New York: D. Van Nostrand Company, Inc., 1950. Mitchell (1910–2007) may be best known as the only man to win the Bermuda Race three times, but also as the only one to do it in three consecutive races. But he spent most of his time cruising—gunkholing he called it—and along the way he became a very good marine photographer. In this book he passes along some of what he learned about taking pictures of boats and waterscape.

Moitessier, Bernard. *A Sea Vagabond's World.* Dobbs Ferry, NY: Sheridan House, 1998. Moitessier (1925–1994), born into a French Indochina colonial family, ran away to sea as a youth in a homemade sailboat. He was a spiritualist who felt the sea as home. He famously abandoned the first around-the-world singlehanded race by veering away from the finish line in England to sail another halfway around the world to his home in Tahiti. His intimacy with the sea may have underlain the carelessness that caused him to lose three of his boats to the beach. After losing his *Joshua* at Cabo San Lucas he went to San Francisco, where we built his last boat, *Tomata,* at Sanford Wood. The cited volume is one of his many books.

Plumber, Henry M. *Me, the Boy, and the Cat.* Rye, NH: Cyrus Chandler Company, 1961. Plumber well describes a fine voyage in the Cape Cod catboat *Mascot* from New Bedford to Miami and back during the winter of 1912/1913. This kind of voyaging is not what the Cape Cod cats were developed for, but Plumber's voyage does show their versatility and the privilege that shoal draft grants the cruiser.

Stackpole, Edouard A. *Life Saving Nantucket*. Nantucket Lifesaving
    Museum, 1972. Stackpole, the historian of Nantucket whaling,
    recounts the best stories of shipwreck and lifesaving off the Island.

Starbuck, Alexander. *The History of Nantucket*. Boston: C. E.
    Goodspeed & Co., 1924. A scholarly tome offering a documentary
    history of the Island.

Tompkins, Jane. *Two Pennies Overboard*. Nantucket: The Homestead,
    1976. This volume is a reprint of the 1948 edition published by J.
    B. Lippincott Company. It is a children's story of an inadvertent
    voyage taken in a Rainbow. Like most children's stories it has a
    happy ending and a moral: always throw your pennies overboard
    at Brant Point when leaving the Island.

U. S. Department of Commerce, Coast and Geodetic Survey. *Tidal
    Current Charts, Narragansett Bay to Nantucket Sound, Third
    Edition*. Rockville, MD: n.d. (ca. 1960). This publication no longer
    seems to be available, but it is reproduced in *Eldridge*, pp. 66–77.
    A necessity for sailing the Sound.

Whipple, A. B. C., *Vintage Nantucket*. Chester, CT: Globe Pequot
    Press, 1978. A collection of memories of time on Nantucket.

White, Robert Eldridge, Jr. *Eldridge Tide and Pilot Book 2013*.
    Medfield, MA: Author, 2013. Published annually for the past 140
    years, *Eldridge* is an almanac of tide and current with lots of
    useful nautical lore added in.

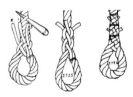

Eye splice

GAZETTEER

MAP PAGE	PLACE NAME	LATITUDE	LONGITUDE	PAGE REFERENCE
54	Abrams Point	41–17.75N	70–03.86W	107
100	Bass Point Bar	41–19.41N	70–01.49W	99
54	Bass Point	41–19.41N	70–02.04W	98–100, 103
36	Bass Rip	41–18N	69–56W	43
36	Bearse Shoal			42
112	Bigalow Point	41–18, 93N	70–19.99W	122
112	Bonita Bar	41–17.05N	70–14, 31W	119, 123, 134, 142, 148
63	Brant Point	41–17.41N	70–05, 41W	16, 25, 61, 64, 68, 70, 73, 74, 79, 82, 88, 130, 146
36	Butler Hole	41–32.3N	69–59.5W	38, 42
36	Cape Pogue	41–25.24N	70–27.11W	38, 41, 44, 45
36	Chappaquiddick	41–22.5N	70.28.6W	38, 44, 45, 113
	Chord of the Bay	41–21N	70–04W	49, 51, 52, 142
54	Coatue	41–18N	70–03W	8, 15, 16, 51, 58, 60, 61, 68, 81, 86–99, 101–103, 106, 107, 142
54	Coatue Beach	41–18N	70–03.2W	14, 58, 87, 142
63	Coatue Point	41–17.88N	70–05.66W	58, 65, 88–92
78	Commercial Wharf	41–16.98N	70–05.66W	77, 79
54	Coskata	41–21.1N	70–01.1W	15, 52, 54, 58, 86, 89, 102, 141
100	Coskata Beach	41–21.3N	70–01.6W	58, 59
100	Coskata Bluff	41–20.9N	70–00.7W	61, 101
100	Coskata Creek	41–20.8N	70–01.2W	81, 102
100	Coskata Pond	41–21.1N	70–00.9W	28, 102
36	Cross Rip Shoal	41–26.5N	70–17.5W	35, 38, 40–42, 45
104	East Polpis Harbor	41–21.3N	70–02.6W	105
112	East Pond	41–18.2N	70–14.7W	17, 48, 133
36	Eel Point	41–17.36N	70–12.36W	15, 16, 45, 111, 113, 115–117, 119, 122, 123, 130, 132, 133, 137, 148
112	Esthers Island	41–17.1N	70–11.8W	119, 120
54	First Bight	41–18N	70–04.6W	83, 93, 96
54	First Point	41–17.57N	70–04.79W	73, 83, 87, 89, 90, 92, 94

MAP PAGE	PLACE NAME	LATITUDE	LONGITUDE	PAGE REFERENCE
54	Five Fingered Deep	41–18.2N	70–03.3W	73, 83, 95, 96, 106
54	Five Fingered Point	41–18.91N	70–02.71W	82, 88, 97, 98
54	Folger Marsh	41–17.6N	70–02.6W	107
78	Great Harbor YC	41–16.76N	70–05.52W	80
36	Great Point	41–23.51N	70–03.06W	8, 16, 17, 33, 37–39, 42–44, 51, 52, 56, 57, 58, 65, 68, 86, 91, 102, 133, 137, 139, 141, 142
36	Great Round Shoal	41–28N	69–55W	17, 22, 38, 40, 42, 44, 141
36	Handkerchief Shoal	41–31N	70–03W	
54	Haulover	41–20.7N	70–00.6W	61, 101, 102, 133
36	Hawes Shoal	41–25N	70–23.5W	45, 46
54	Head of the Harbor	41–19.9N	70–00.9W	73, 82, 83, 96, 99–103, 147
112	Hither Creek	41–16.5N	70–11.9W	113, 116–119, 122, 133
63	Hook Pool	41–17.72N	70–05.36W	
36	Horseshoe Shoal	41–30N	70–20W	
63	Hussey Shoal			70, 73, 82, 106
36	Long Shoal	41–24N	70–20W	
36	Madaket	41–16.5N	70–11.6W	2, 116–119, 122, 132, 137, 139
114	Madaket Harbor	41–17.0N	70–12.2W	17, 48, 111, 115, 116, 123
36	Miacomet Rip	41–14N	70–06W	138–140
63	Monomoy	41–16.9N	70–04.5W	69, 106, 107
36	Monomoy Island	41–35N	69–59.5W	24, 37, 38, 42
36	Monomoy Shoals			38
36	Muskeget	41–20.1N	70–17.9W	22, 45, 111, 113, 122, 126, 127
36	Muskeget Channel			21, 37, 38, 40, 44–46, 111, 122, 134
36	Muskeget Rock	41–20.1N	70–23.3W	113
36	Mutton Shoal	41–19.6N	70–25W	21, 38, 44, 45, 113
36	Nantucket Bar	41–18.2N	70–07W	4, 15, 51, 58, 59, 61, 62, 64, 92
78	Nantucket YC	41–17.18N	70–05.85W	79, 96
112	North Point	41–17.8N	70–11.87W	114, 130, 132, 133
112	North Pond	41–18.6N	70–16.5W	17, 33
36	Norton Shoal	41–25.5N	70–21.0W	
36	Old Man Shoal	41–13N	69–59W	44, 139
78	Old North Wharf	41–17.09N	70–05.75W	64, 77, 79
78	Old South Wharf	41–16.98N	70–05.64W	77
63	Pimneys Point	41–17.39N	70–04.30W	107
54	Pocomo Bight	41–19.3N	70–02.6W	83, 87, 96–99, 103
54	Pocomo Head	41–18.81N	70–01.85W	83, 98, 103
54	Pocomo Point	41–19.01N	70–02.00W	83, 96, 99, 102–104
36	Point Rip	41–24.2N	70–02.7W	42–44, 56, 139, 141, 142
36	Pollock Rip	41–32.5N	69–56W	25, 38, 40–42, 45
54	Polpis	41–17.9N	70–00.9W	2, 83, 104–106

MAP PAGE	PLACE NAME	LATITUDE	LONGITUDE	PAGE REFERENCE
54	Quaise	41–17.87N	70–02.06W	107
36	Rose and Crown	41–20N	69–46W	43
36	Sconset	41–15.8N	69–57.8W	25, 33, 44, 139, 140
54	Second Bight	41–18.4N	70–03.7W	93–96
54	Second Point	41–18.11N	70–03.96W	70, 73, 83, 93–96, 99
63	Shimmo	41–17.2N	70–04.4W	72, 106
54	Shimmo Creeks	41–17.25N	70–04.11W	81, 107
36	Shovelful Shoal	41–23N	70–18W	
36	Smith Point	41–17.08N	70–14.00W	16, 17, 40, 111, 115–117, 119–123, 132–134, 139
54	Squam Head	41–19.1N	69–59.3W	25, 140
78	Steamboat Wharf	41–17.15N	70–05.77W	73, 74, 79
78	Straight Wharf	41–17.08N	70–05.66W	74, 78
63	The Creeks	41–16.6N	70–05.4W	16, 28, 73, 80, 106–109
63	The Cut	41–17.96N	70–05.63W	12, 58, 65, 73, 90, 91
36	The Galls	41–22.5N	70–01.7W	17, 39, 52, 54, 58, 86
63	The Hook	41–17.70N	70–05.47W	65, 89–92
63	The Horseshed	41–17.5N	70–05.2W	68, 90, 92
63	The Jetties	41–17.80N	70–06.28W	
112	The Lagoon	41–17.5N	70–14.9W	16, 119, 122, 123, 130, 134, 135, 137, 148
54	Third Bight	41–18.8N	70–03.1W	96–98
61	Third Point	41–18.46N	70–03.36W	83, 87, 94–97
36	Tom Nevers Head	41–14.62N	69–59.45W	44, 138, 139
78	Town Boat Ramp	41–17.27N	70–05.82W	
63	Town Deep	41–17.2N	70–05.4W	73
78	Town Dock	41–16.92N	70–05.61W	
36	Tuckernuck	41–19N	70–15W	16–17, 21–23, 37–39, 111, 113, 115–116, 118, 120–123, 130, 133–134, 137
36	Tuckernuck Bank	41–19N	70–15W	38, 45, 119, 127, 132, 134
36	Tuckernuck Shoal	41–24N	70–14W	38–41, 45
112	Warrens Landing	41–17.11N	70–11.51W	
36	Wasque Point	41–21.15N	70–27.04W	
36	Wasque Shoal	41–19N	70–26W	33, 45
54	Wauwinet	41–19.75N	69–59.80W	25, 61, 73, 75, 81–83, 101–103, 140, 141, 148
104	West Polpis Harbor	41–17.9N	70–01.4W	105, 106
112	Whale Point	41–17.3N	70–14.81W	119
54	Wyers Bight	41–19.8N	70–02.1W	87, 98, 99
54	Wyers Point	41–19.91N	70–01.83W	87, 88, 95, 99–101

ACKNOWLEDGMENTS

Nat philbrick and dick duncan of Mill Hill Press performed an act of great faith when they asked me to write this book. It was a book I had thought about for years but would never have started without their explicit request and support. I was an untried writer, for whom "C+" was a best grade in prep school English. Mill Hill Press publishes books of local interest to Nantucket and is willing to lose money on titles it believes important. That Nat and Dick would chose me to lose money on gave me the confidence to begin.

Their support included bringing in Cecile Kaufman, who created from my text and sketches the beautiful volume you hold in your hands. Each decision she made along the way created beauty and surprise. Nat and Dick also brought along Judith Brown to copy-edit, a process I was unfamiliar with. She prevented my twelve chapters from being written in twelve different styles. She established consistency throughout the text.

Only after the work was all done did I realize that many of the contributors were shipmates who had sailed aboard *Impala* with me. Nat Philbrick made his first ocean passage aboard. Garth Grimmer and Connor Wallace, the photographers, are old *Impala* hands. Their photographs speak for themselves. Jim Powers is an exception. He never sailed aboard, but his telephoto shot from

Jetties Beach of *Impala* leaving for Europe that cold, gale-struck May morning is among the best ever taken of her. Oliver LaFarge, whom Connor brought aboard *Impala* in 2004, reintroduced me to his fellow Tuckernucker, Richard Limeburner, who himself had sailed aboard *Impala* back in the 1980s when she was new to me. Richard is the brains behind the first half of chapter four. Eric Holch, whose flags illustrate the Beaufort Scale, has been sailing and racing *Impala* for as long as I have had her. Not only did these friends contribute their work, but also it was from decades of sailing and talking with them around the cabin table that the substance of the book derives.

All good friends indeed. But the one whose insistence countervailed the doubt imbued at Exeter Academy so many years ago and who actually made the work possible is my lady Sandra. She read the early versions and forced me to accept their merit. From then on, writing the book was a pleasure. I hope that, for you the reader, reading it is too.

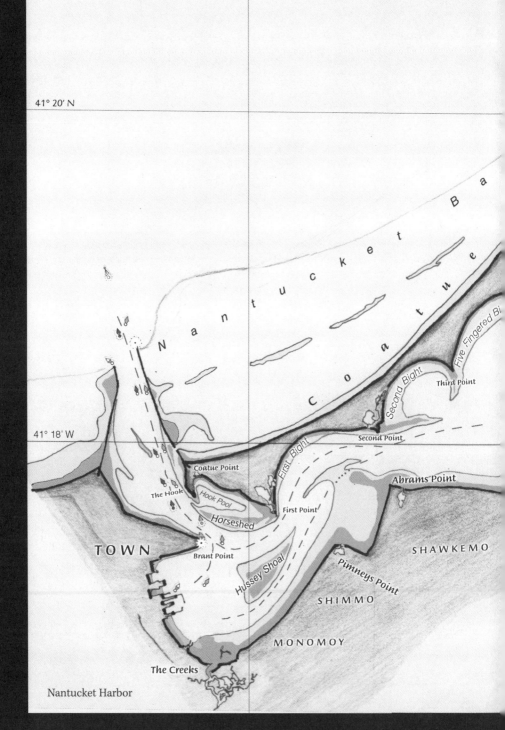

70° 05' W

41° 20' N

41° 18' W

Nantucket Ba

Coatue

Five Fingered Bi

Third Point

Second Bight

Second Point

First Bight

Coatue Point

Abrams Point

The Hook

Hook Pool

First Point

Horseshed

SHAWKEMO

TOWN

Brant Point

Hussey Shoal

Pimneys Point

SHIMMO

MONOMOY

The Creeks

Nantucket Harbor